THE
PASTOR'S SECRETARY

What Really Happens Behind Closed Doors

THE
PASTOR'S SECRETARY

What Really Happens Behind Closed Doors

WENDI HAYMAN

Glory to Glory
PUBLICATIONS

The Pastor's Secretary
Copyright © 2018 by Wendi Hayman

Scripture quotations are taken from the *Holy Bible*, King James Ver-
sion/Amplified Parallel Edition, copyright © 1995 by The Zondervan
Corporation and the Lockman Foundation. All rights reserved.

Scripture quotations (NIV) are taken from the *Holy Bible*, New International Version, copyright © 1973, 1978, 1984 by International Bible
Society. The Zondervan Corporation. All rights reserved.

Scripture quotations (NLT) are taken from the *Holy Bible*, New Living
Translation, copyright © 1886, 2004, 2015 by Tyndale House Foundation. Used by permission of Tyndale House Publishers, LLC Inc., Car-
ol Stream, Illinois 60188. All rights reserved.

Printed in the United States of America
First Printing, 2019
ISBN 978-0-9982435-5-9
Published by:
Glory to Glory Publications, LLC
glorytoglorypublications@gmail.com
www.GlorytoGloryPublications.com
www.WendiHayman.com

Cover Design: Ed Wolfe at blazingcovers@gmail.com
Interior Design: Glory to Glory Publications, LLC
Editor: Emerald Garnett Editing and English & Sign Language Mas-
ters, LLC

This is a work of creative nonfiction. The events are of the author's
life and experiences. While all the stories in this book are true, some
names and identifying details used were to recreate events, locales,
and conversations from memories of them and are in no way meant
to defame any person or place.

I dedicate this book to the loving memory of my father,
Caleb Morrow, Jr.
Daddy, you always believed in me, and you told me when I was
just a teenager that I was supposed to be a writer.
Although it took 30 plus years, I became just what you said I
would be because it was ultimately God's purpose for my life.
This is my third book Daddy and I believe that the spirit of your
words spoken to me all those years ago continue to resonate to keep
me going in my life's purpose.
Love, your Baby Girl!

Let's Stay Connected
Follow me on

TABLE OF CONTENTS

PREFACE

Let me tell you. I had gotten myself in a whole mess, just jacked all the way up. I was doing dumb stuff for a 40+ year old, married woman. My life had gotten to a point where I let someone else's actions and response cause me to make bad decisions. These were decisions to do what I wanted to do without thinking about the repercussions. These decisions caused me to truly let my flesh take over, get the best of me, and make a fool of me.

I put myself in a position to let men use me for their own selfishness and personal satisfaction. Although, I made myself believe it was also for my benefit, I knew they were using me. They were all married. I was too. There was no way they could have any real interest in me or that I could have anything further with them, beyond what we were doing with one another. Who was I fooling? Too much was at stake; they had too much to lose.

The decisions I made also caused me to lose a lot, but instead, I thought I was gaining. I lost my self-dignity, value, worth, virtue, faith, and relationships. I lost my mind and my peace of mind. I was completely driven and controlled by my flesh and nothing mattered. Not only did I not worry about how my marriage would be affected, I didn't even stop to think about how the things I was doing as a married, Christian woman appeared to my teenage daughter.

I was hurt, angry, bitter, and broken. But how did I get there? Interestingly enough, this reminded me of my past, but this time should have been different because now I was a Christian. Before, when I felt lonely, rejected, unloved, and undervalued, I would run to other men. But this time, as a married, Christian woman, and instead of running to other men, I should have run to God.

I knew my husband loved me, and I will never doubt that, but he hurt me deeply in the beginning of our marriage and I never recovered. He was an extremely hard worker and truly a giver. Not just to me, but also to so many others. As the years went on, that's kind of what got in the way. He was giving his time, himself, and money to those outside of the house more than to his family in his home. He expressed his love to me in his own way rather than according to my love language, which was quality time. As a result, during the duration of my marriage, I spent more time alone than I wanted.

Our big house just didn't comfort me when I was most often there by myself, especially after our daughter went off to college. My luxury Mercedes Benz didn't bring me an abundance of joy because I was driving it all alone. All the designer clothes, shoes, and handbags that filled my massive closet couldn't give me companionship when I needed it; they couldn't give me conversation, reassurance, or the quality time I so longed for from the one I was married to.

Even though I looked darn good on the outside, on the inside I was torn, broken, hurting, bitter, miserable, lost, and lonely. Even though my house, with its beautiful stone and stucco material, was gorgeous from the outside, it was cold, dreary, empty, and lonely on the inside. I didn't even have anyone who I could call my friend to fill the gap of the massive amount of loneliness I was subjected to throughout the years. Yes, I had my daughter, but as she grew up, she wanted her own time and space. She couldn't be the quality time fill-in for her daddy forever. At times, I found myself envying her friendships because I wanted friends too.

After going through all that you'll read in this story, in the end, I died. Not a physical death. But I died to the pride and foolishness I was operating in at the time. I died to the self-righteous and judgmental person I had become and mastered, one who was good at throwing stones while living in sin. More importantly, I died to the dictates of my flesh. After all the junk in me died, I was able to live, I mean really live.

Before this part of me died, I thought I was living because I had a husband who had a prominent career, who would buy me almost anything, and who would take me lots of places. I thought I was living because I had the big house that drew attention, admiration, acceptance, and applause from everyone who visited, along with the oooh's and aah's at the beautifully decorated interior, of which I was the creative genius. I thought I was living because I drove a Mercedes Benz S550 with a distinct color that commanded attention as I drove it down the street or pulled it into spaces and places. I really thought I was living. Truth be told, I didn't know what living was until I got free of all the demons that were living inside of me.

After I died to myself, I became free and alive. It was like I was a new person. I could see better, think clearer, and I was a more genuine, loving and authentic person. So much had changed about me. I was happy about the new person I had become after I let go of the old person and all of the things that I had entangled myself in. My journey to freedom hadn't been easy. It had been a painful and rough period, but I made it through. All it took was me making a decision. But this time, I made the right decision. I made the decision that I no longer wanted to live the lie of a life that I was living. I made the decision that I no longer wanted to be broken, bitter, and miserable, but I wanted to be happy. I made the decision that I no longer wanted to do the wrong things that I was doing, hurting others in the process, but that I wanted to do much better so that I could be an example to others.

It is my prayer that you read this story not through the eyes of judgment or condemnation, but through the eyes of love and with a spirit for healing, wholeness, deliverance, restoration, and more importantly freedom. This all happened many years ago, and I suffered in silence regarding my past until, finally, on August 25, 2018, during my attendance at a conference in Dallas, TX, God gave me the release to tell my story. That is why this book was written.

ACKNOWLEDGMENTS

Just as my other books, this book went through a long, tough labor, even to the point where I wanted to quit, but I thank God for its birth. This book was harder to write than any other because of the transparency in which it contains, however, All the glory goes to my Lord and Savior, Jesus Christ. I thank God for choosing me and my story as a Voice to freedom for those who have suffered in silence, and for giving me the strength and courage to be transparent to write and share my story. It surely wasn't easy, but I must say, so much liberty and freedom was achieved as a result of this writing.

I would like to acknowledge those who believed in me, supported, and encouraged me throughout this process— my girls, Marcia and Donye', my mother, Ora Morrow, my family, friends, and church family. I thank you Donye' for your continuous support and encouragement, but most of all, for saying that I am your Role Model after you saw the end result of what I went through. Thank you Marcia, for being patient, understanding, and dedicated to the beginning of this process with me as first editor, and for always supporting and encouraging me. A special thank you to my mentor and Pastor, Pastor Beverly Mahoney for your continuous prayers, counsel, support, encouragement, and for not joining my pity party's but for sharpening me with the Word. My spiritual mother, Minister Pamela Price for always being there when I needed you, praying, being a listening ear, a voice of reason, and always imparting the word of God in me when I needed it the most. Thank you to my siblings, Jennifer, John, Ethel, Odetta, Grace, and Ro for all of your love, encouragement, prayers, conversations, and support. Thank you to my Editor, Danita Brooks for joining me on the last leg of this journey. I know it wasn't easy and I was a tough client, but thank you for seeing it through to the end, telling my story with total clarity for the end result- Freedom.

I especially want to thank my Facebook and Instagram friends and followers who encouraged me throughout this entire book process, especially when I endured persecution for this story and the very risqué excerpts I posted. Thank you Dana Eure for every post comment and Inbox message you sent to encourage me continuously, and for praying me through this journey.

To anyone who I did not specifically name, but you have supported me, encouraged me, and prayed for me, I would like to thank you and know that you are loved.

"And you shall know the truth, and the truth shall make you free."
"If the Son therefore shall make you free, you shall be free indeed."
(John 8:32, 36)

This story was written for **freedom**. Freedom from sin, secrets, silence, and shame. Freedom from bondage and strongholds. Freedom from the types of leaders and members, men and women, who take advantage of members within the congregation. Freedom for those who are victims of this type of behavior and who have to suffer in silence. Freedom from ministries and cults that keep you bound and blocked from deliverance from sin. Freedom from assumptions and speculations. Freedom to know that, although you may not want to believe it, the inappropriate behavior you observed or discerned was probably really happening. Freedom from past issues and traumas that shape your identity, causing you to make decisions against God's will for your life.

INTRODUCTION

I know that this story is going to make me sound like a hoe, whore, hoochie, trash, or whatever demeaning name you can imagine. At the same time, I can honestly say that my actions were completely fueled by low self-esteem, insignificance, rejection issues, hurt, and brokenness. I was also heavily influenced by the perverse spirit of lust that had me bound. Consequently, I can accept being called all of those things regarding my behavior back then because that's not who I am anymore. That's what I did, but it is not who I am.

Now, **"I am Free!"** First off, I thank God for His love, forgiveness, grace, and mercy, but most importantly, I thank Him for His deliverance and restoration. Secondly, I was not in this alone. The other parties involved were also cohorts and influencers of the behaviors we exhibited with one another. No, I was NOT strong enough to resist the temptation, especially from the vulnerable place I was in at that time: years prior, I had experienced infidelity in my marriage when my husband was unfaithful, and I did not get proper counseling or heal properly from the situation. The remnants of that traumatic experience were seeds that had lain dormant in me until the time had come for a harvest to be reaped.

When seeds are sown, they are eventually harvested. The *seed*—my husband's infidelity—went through the full process of harvest as according to Mark 4:28. *First the blade,* me entertaining the advances and flirtations of other men, *then the ear,* my involvement in inappropriate behavior with church members and the Pastor; and finally *after that the full corn in the ear,* committing adultery.

During marriage counseling, my husband and I had to listen to a teaching series pertaining to dating and marriage. In the teaching, the Pastor said, "Be careful of the seeds you give a woman because she takes it, incubates it, and gives it back to you bigger than what you gave her. If you sow hate or mistreatment into her, she'll give it back to you greater. But if you want a vision to grow, plant that seed in a woman and see what she gives you back."

In my case, my husband gave me the seed of infidelity. I received that seed with devastation to know that he'd been with another woman in the first year of our marriage. For years, I incubated the tragedy of this happening in my new marriage and didn't share it with many others except the Pastor and his wife for the sake of counseling, and a friend who allowed me to escape to her home to recover from the initial shock. Unfortunately, I gave him back an abundant harvest, a hefty crop from the seed he gave to me.

To help set the stage for what you're about to read, I want to start off with a few definitions.

Subtle
Making use of clever and indirect methods to achieve something.

Genesis 3:1
Now the serpent was more <u>subtle</u> than any beast of the field which the Lord God had made. And he said unto the woman…

I didn't come on to the Pastor and he didn't come on to me. It all started with the **subtle** joke that he made with a sexual undertone (*Genesis 3:1 and he said unto the woman*), that I responded back with my own sexual undertone (*Gene-*

sis 3:2 And the woman said unto the serpent). I had taken the bait….(Genesis 3:6 *And when the woman saw that the tree was good for food, and that it was pleasant to the eyes…).*

Affair

An affair is a sexual relationship, romantic friendship, *or* passionate attachment between two people without the attached person's significant other knowing.

An affair is also a romantic and emotionally intense sexual or emotional relationship.
Typically, and with a few exceptions, an affair is considered a betrayal of trust.
A platonic relationship can be called a romantic affair as well.

An emotional affair, is one that lacks sexual intimacy but has intense or enduring emotional intimacy.

A cyber affair, is one that has emotional and/or sexual undertones. This is accomplished via chat, webcam, email, text, and other technology-based mediums.

**What went on with the Pastor and me can be identified in all these definitions of an affair.
Perception

Perception is the ability to see, hear, or become aware of something through the senses, a way of regarding, understanding, or interpreting something; a mental impression.

On occasion, during conversations the Pastor would make the statement to me, "Your perception is your own reality," and I never understood why he kept saying that. Then one Sunday after we were no longer involved, he taught a message entitled, *Your perception is your own reality.* I strongly know that this message was taught to cover up the basis of what had actually taken place, with me.

For example, when we were behind closed doors, hugging closely for an extended period of time, and I would think, "He must really like me." Anyone I shared this thought with would question my thinking. "Because he gave me a hug that really lingered," I would reply. If anyone told the Pastor, "She says you like her because of the way you hugged her," and he would respond, "That's just her perception."

During the teaching, I received revelation that if the truth was ever exposed regarding his actions with me or anyone else, people will be able to make the automatic response that it was only the individual's perception of his interactions with them. I know that we spent a whole lot of time *behind closed doors* behaving inappropriately. In fact, if I was to ever say we had an affair, I would believe he would say that it was *my perception* of the things we did that made me think it was an affair. Therefore, I will detail many of the actions that went on and then you tell me what your perception is.

CHAPTER 1

New Member

If you've been saved, a Christian, going to church, praying, and reading your bible for any number of years, you become familiar with the voice of God and promptings of Holy Spirit. When we don't follow the leading of Holy Spirit, we just may find ourselves in places and situations that we were never meant to be in. Holy Spirit is like an alarm that goes off when something is wrong, we're heading in the wrong direction, or we're entering into a wrong place. Once we have the thought, "I'm not supposed to be here," we often think it's too late for us to get out, we discern incorrectly and stay, and/or we get counsel and advice that God did not intend for our personal situation. 1 Corinthians 10:13 says, *"No temptation has overtaken you except what is common to mankind. And God is faithful; he will not let you be tempted beyond what you can bear. But when you are tempted he will also provide a way out so that you can endure it."* This means that when we find ourselves in temptations and situations that we shouldn't be in, God's word promises that He will provide a way to escape so that we are able to handle the exit. We have to be in tune with Holy Spirit, so that when He is showing us the way out, we will recognize it and take it. Oftentimes, we get into wrong situations or stay there too long, putting ourselves through unnecessary stresses and pains because we didn't escape when He was showing us the way out, or telling us not to go there in the first place.

How I wish I had heeded Holy Spirit's warning. Prior to me ever meeting the man who I later married, I received a warning that I remember clearly to this day because it haunted me for years, throughout my entire marriage. Even though I knew the scripture that tells us to cast our cares unto the Lord— and I did so every time the warning would come to the forefront of my mind during turbulent times in my marriage— I would pray, rebuke the thought, or replace it with other thoughts. But for some reason it kept coming up.

A man I had previously been engaged to called me and said, "God told me to tell you, do not marry the person you plan to marry. If you do, you will live in years of turmoil." Well, I didn't heed the warning for two reasons. The first reason is that I perceived it as jealousy of a former fiancè, a self-proclaimed Prophet, with whom I had broken up with years prior. He had just appeared out of the blue to my mother's house and asked her to call me because he need-ed to warn me. The second reason was because, at the time he gave me the warning, I was not even dating anyone, let alone planning to get married. As a matter of fact, at that time, I was done with the idea of marriage and even dating, especially "Christian dating," because my relation-ship with him had failed. Oh how that later changed. But I didn't heed the warning and got married a couple of years later to the next man with whom I'd gotten into a serious relationship.

I had previously met my husband's Pastor, the Pastor's wife, and other church members at the same time I met him for the first time. Because we met online, when my hus-band and I were initially talking, I learned that his church attended a conference at the church I was a member of for several years. Once we started dating, I visited the state where he lived and also his church on several occasions. I even went to a holiday gathering at the Pastor's house during one visit. The church was fairly new and small, having been in existence for only a couple of years. At the time, I was attending a vastly popular megachurch and the idea of having to "downsize" in churches was not appealing to me.

After I got married and moved to another state to live with my husband, I expressed to him that I did not want to go to that church. He told me that I did not have a choice because husbands and wives go to the same church. I expressed to him that in the church I previously attended, I personally knew two ladies who had long-term marriages and neither of their husbands attended the same church as they did. He was not having it. I was told I had to go, and I begrudgingly went. To this day, I can say that I never officially "joined the church" by going up front during the altar call for church membership. So basically, I was forced into becoming a member by marriage. Once again, I had exerted myself to fit into a place I didn't belong; the marriage apparently because of the warning, and the church to appease my husband, especially since we were newlyweds.

For a long time, I felt like I did not belong at the new church I had to go to. I never felt like I fit in. Although I got heavily involved in working and serving, deep down I felt out of place. Yet, just like I had done in my past, I exerted myself to fit into a place and in relationships I wasn't supposed to be in to appease others or so that I wouldn't have to endure rejection.

Although I had initially fellowshipped with the Pastor and his wife and concluded that they were cool, nice people, after really getting to know him, I didn't really care too much for him. I thought he was very arrogant, but he masqueraded it as being "confident, and knowing who he is in Christ," yada yada. This, too, was my husband's personality, the reason for which many people disliked him. Since I had come out of a huge, megachurch, this new Pastor, his church, and his teachings were elementary to me. I felt like I was already in college, spiritually. Well, actually I was because I had been a member of a strong faith-based ministry for 6 years, completed 3 years of Bible College and Ministry Development, graduated and had my Minister's License. I didn't disclose this to them though. Besides they were attending Church Development conferences at the ministry where I was a member at the time. In addition, I was pretty far along in my spiritual knowledge. Pridefully, I was convinced that I knew more of the word than this man and "What can he teach me?" In fact, it took me a long time to warm up to the ministry and to the Pastor. I'll admit that I was pretty bitter about having to attend a "small" church. Initially, I didn't really allow the word that was being taught to take root in me. Eventually, I started to be more attentive to the teachings to make them applicable to my life.

Since I didn't know anyone in the new state I had moved to, my husband thought it would be good if I became friends with the Pastor's wife, especially since he and the Pastor were friends and she had previously been friends with his ex-wife. I tried and it wasn't an easy task. She was an extremely guarded woman, not as easy to get close to as her husband was. They welcomed me, were nice to me, tried to embrace me, but it wasn't a close embrace, mainly not from her. I gathered that was probably since she knew the full story of my husband's ex-wife prior to me. The two had worked together, were friends, but the ex-wife started having an affair with a male co-worker and left him. Also, rumor was that she and the Pastor messed around as well; of course this has been denied by both the Pastor and his wife.

The part of the story many people didn't know is that my husband had an affair on that wife, who was his second one, and his first wife too. I guess "affairs begat affairs." Or as the saying goes "hurt people, hurt people." This is so true. And this vicious cycle in marriages and relationships has to stop. Someone has to take a stand and say, *"I'm going to maintain the value of integrity in my marriage and my covenant with my spouse."* It would have been nice if that could have been me, and it could have been had I received the help that I was crying out for after my husband's infidelity. I received counseling here and there, but it wasn't sustainable. Because instead, what I later received was a predator to my vulnerability and weakness, which shifted some things in me and my thinking. I even had thoughts like "Well, if a Pastor can act like this and God still use him and blesses him, and I'm just a pew member, surely the Lord will bless me." (slaps forehead) I know, crazy thinking!

The Pastor's wife and I would hang out intermittently to shop, have lunch, or dinner, and attend conferences, only at my request. We would talk on the phone, but only if I called. Eventually, I received a two-year temporary assignment at the company she worked at so I thought we would at least hang out at lunch, but that didn't happen. Basically, we only really communicated when I did church work and needed her feedback, approval, and permission to have materials printed. She hardly ever reached out to me on her own. Moreover, the relationship that my husband hoped she and I would have never happened.

Despite other times, this marriage included, where I put myself in relationships where I didn't belong, this time I listened to my mother who always told me not to kiss anybody's butt—well, not exactly the word "butt," if you know what I mean. One day, many years later, the Pastor mentioned to me that his wife and I should have been friends. When I told him that I tried to years prior, and it didn't happen, he had the nerve to say to me, "You didn't try hard enough." I was taken aback by his response. I said when a person wants to be in a relationship, what is given is reciprocated back and she didn't reciprocate. To me, that spoke volumes, so I moved on.

Because I had rejection issues at the time, the rejection I experienced from her caused me to feel some type of way about her and I dealt with her on a minimal basis. I give an in-depth account of my low self-esteem and rejection issues in my book *Blind Ambition*. I encourage you to grab a copy of this book to learn more about that part of me and how I got free from rejection.

So, I said to myself, "If she doesn't want to be my friend, then I will be friends with her husband," and that, I did. As a result, I started to let down my wall with him. If you know anything about people who have rejection issues, you know that they keep a wall of defense all around their heart, not allowing many people in. This was even a tough wall for my husband to get around, but he managed to do it temporarily during our dating phase. That was when he truly showed me love and kindness, but it eventually faded after we were married.

Since I was forced to attend this church, I guessed I had to make the most of it and become involved. After about 6 months of being there, I talked with the Pastor concerning my administrative and creative skills. I shared with him some things that I knew hands-on from the megachurch that I felt could be helpful to the ministry. In an effort to help the church advance, expand, and do more, I took to the Pastor what I saw and learned in the megachurch to help them implement the information that was learned from attending the church development conferences so the church could become more current and forward-moving. Some things were rejected and some things were accepted. Since I had rejection issues and didn't understand that my idea was being rejected and not me, I became defensive and combative. I would explode and he and I would have heated arguments, both publicly where other congregants including his wife witnessed, and many in private as well.

The way I got involved working in the ministry is by re-inventing the church's newsletter. I emulated the design from my old church and tailored it to the new church. He liked most of my ideas. It was a monthly newsletter with announcements and a "Pastor's Corner." I wrote all the content and utilized graphics; however, he had to approve it. So, that's how we initially started working together. It wasn't a close working relationship; it was just as platonic as he was with his other leaders. The newsletter became my project and I worked diligently to make it as professional as possible.

Then, I started helping the Pastor out with some administrative tasks. I was an Administrative Assistant in my workplace, which made this come natural for me. Later, I eventually became known, unofficially, as the Pastor's Assistant. I was never formally given that title. Due to my creative gift and graphic design background, which I learned in college, I started designing more church products: CD covers, visitor's packets, flyers, postcards, and banners. At that point, my official title was Leader of Marketing and Publications. I did those duties along with the administrative work I did for the Pastor. I even created the content for the church's first professionally designed website, and I maintained the content regularly. All of this required the Pastor's approval before anything could be released, which caused us to have to work together more frequently.

I worked my day job and would come home and do church work. Sometimes I would even do church work at my job. While at home, I spent more time working on church stuff for the Pastor and less time with my husband. The Pastor and I spent a lot of time on the telephone, all hours of the day and night, when we were working on content or a special project. This frustrated my husband. He'd often refer to the Pastor as my second husband, which I denied because it wasn't true...at the time. As time went on, there were even some members who witnessed our interactions around church, referred to the Pastor as my second husband. Someone even told my husband that the rumor on the street was that in order to get to Pastor, people had to go through me.

After services, I would go to my office and get to work and stay until several hours later. I can say that I literally "jumped through hoops" for the Pastor and ministry. But pretty much everyone who was on the leadership team did, and even some volunteer ministry workers, because none of us were paid employees. "You're always working," people would always say to me, and it was true. I became dedicated to my work and the Pastor.

I had also served as back-up armor bearer to the Pastor's wife. I was to become her assistant too, and she and I discussed this. But it was just talk, and she never indoctrinated me into the role...not even after her husband encouraged her to increase the amount of responsibility she gave me so that I could work more with her than with him. I wonder if I had been allowed to work with her more, would have possibly stopped the affair that was brewing between him and me. We will never know.

Ever since I moved to my new city, it seemed I could only get temporary jobs. I never understood why, but in the interim, this gave me the flexibility to work at the church when I was between temp assignments.

CHAPTER 2

The Seed

The Bible states in Galatians 6:7-10 (NIV) *"Do not be deceived; God cannot be mocked. A man reaps what he sows. Whoever sows to please their flesh, from the flesh will reap destruction; whoever sows to please the Spirit, from the Spirit will reap eternal life. Let us not become weary in doing good, for at the proper time we will reap a harvest if we do not give up. Therefore, as we have opportunity, let us do good to all people, especially to those who belong to the family of believers."* **Seed** is defined as the cause or latent beginning of a feeling, process, or condition; cause (something) to begin to develop or grow.

Seeds are sown into us all the time, and we, too, sow seeds into others. We have to be careful with both. Additionally, how you water the seeds determines how they will grow. If the seeds are watered with the wrong things through what we meditate on, focus on, or speak, the seed will develop into the wrong things showing up in our lives. If the seeds are watered with the right things that we meditate on, which is the word of God, and we cast out the wrong thoughts of the wrong seeds by speaking positively, especially the word of God, we will grow and develop into the right thing for our lives.

I have to admit, the reason this story is even at the point

of where it is being told is because when wrong seeds were sown into me, I didn't cast them out. I meditated on those wrong seeds day and night versus the word of God; especially the seed of my husband's infidelity. Psalm 1:2 (AMP) states, *"But his delight is in the law of the Lord, And on His law [His precepts and teachings] he [habitually] meditates day and night."* Therefore, new seeds, such as sexual conversations, that were sown into me, influenced the behaviors in this story because I mediated upon them, especially for an extended period of time. Then I found myself acting out what I mediated on, which led me down the wrong path.

Several of those seeds had to do with my thoughts about the men in that church. Despite the other ways I was initially unimpressed with the church, the one thing it did have were some good looking men; single and married. There were two particular individuals who were just absolutely good looking to me; I was totally attracted to them. I don't know if they felt the same way about me at first, but we were friendly and cordial when we saw one another at church.

I mentioned before that my self-esteem was very low then. I didn't like what I saw when I looked in the mirror. It's not that I thought I was ugly, it's because I defined my looks based on what others said about me—based on the seeds they had planted in me. During my childhood, my siblings and family members on my mother's side teased me about my nose because it was larger than everyone else's. I inherited my nose from my father's side. As a result, I defined my beauty based on my nose. Every time I looked in the mirror, my nose was the main thing that I could see. I thought my best features were my eyes and my lips, however, the seeds sown in my childhood regarding my nose had harvested and dominated over any other good features or qualities I had.

My low self-esteem caused me to wear makeup at all times as I got later into my adult years. It got so bad that I wouldn't even go outside to check the mailbox without putting some makeup on so no one would see my natural face. After getting the slightest attention from other men, I began to dress sexy, flirty, and sometimes provocatively, to get the attention of these men. At the time, I couldn't even tell you why I needed the attention of other men besides it being fueled by low self-esteem. My husband even noticed when the way I dressed changed and commented about it, but I blew it off.

My husband always told me I was beautiful and sexy. He preferred me best without makeup or hair weave, especially since I had long, beautiful hair. But, I didn't always accept it when he said it. My self-esteem wouldn't allow me to accept his compliments. I would often tell him, he was only complimenting me because I was his wife. I would even have other people, strangers even, who were meeting me for the first time to tell me that I was beautiful, compliment me on my looks or how I was dressed, but I would offer a non-confident "thank you," partially accepting their compliments. There had been times when after I was complimented, I would look in the mirror to see if I could see exactly what the other person saw when they looked at me. Even when men would flirt with me or try to talk to me, especially attractive men, I would be left perplexed.

Several years after my husband's infidelity, I guess because we never properly dealt with it and didn't get sufficient counseling, you can say I changed. That is also a story I tell in more detail in my book *Blind Ambition*, but for now, you need to know that I was once an exotic dancer, as we called it back in the day. Now, most would say I was a stripper. No matter what you call it, the old flirty, seductive nature in me came alive again. I think this started leading me on a path that I said I never would go down. I had started to get a harvest from seeds planted long ago. It didn't seem to matter that in the beginning of my marriage, I had told my husband that he didn't have to worry about me leaving him for another man like his previous two wives. I had told him that I wouldn't hurt him or have an affair.

Mind you, I made those statements prior to finding out my husband didn't feel the same way about me, and that he had an affair in our first year of marriage.

With one guy in particular, I'll call him member #1, I remember leaving work at the church to go meet his family at a specific location. The entire time while talking to him and *his wife,* I had just been looking at him, clearly showing my interest. He was so good looking to me, so that made me attracted to him, along with his exceptionally outgoing personality. Then, *his wife* went into the building and he came around to the driver's side of my car and asked, "Are you interested in me?" I responded, "Yes." We then exchanged phone numbers, supposedly because he and *his wife* were going out of town and I was keeping their children. She came out of the building with their children, then they were loaded into my car for us to leave.

The next day, he managed to sneak away to call me, disguised as checking on the kids. Our conversation started off with us talking about the children and then it moved into us sharing personal information about ourselves. I told him I thought he was very attractive and that he reminded me of my former best friend. He said he was attracted to me as well. We actually ended up talking for hours. From this initial conversation alone, many seeds were sown by each of us. From that day forth, we talked on the phone, text, and eventually moved to secret meet-ups. In time, he became my new best friend. After a period of time, we transitioned into having cyber-sex via a video app for smart phones. This all occurred because neither of us recognized the seeds that were being sown and how they were appealing to our flesh.

Concerning the other guy I was attracted to, I'll refer to him as member #2, I tried flirting with him but he didn't pick up on it. One time in particular, my husband hired him to cut our grass because he owned a landscaping service. He came to our house one Saturday morning to cut the grass. I was home alone as usual because my husband worked a lot, which was also the reason why someone else had to cut our grass. The grass had gotten extremely high. After he finished cutting the grass, I cooked him dinner. I grilled some chicken breasts and filet mignon steaks. Since I loved Boston Market's sweet potato casserole, I made a similar one with the granola topping and marshmallows, and some green beans. He had a slight cold that day and asked me to make him some hot tea with lemon and honey to go along with his meal. We ate dinner, talked, and he left. He had no clue that I was trying to attract him. Later he told me that he told his wife about the dinner and she responded that it was inappropriate and I most likely was trying to come on to him. He stated he didn't even recognize it as that.

Sometime later, one day after church, I saw him sitting alone, playing a game on his iPad while he waited for his wife. I made small talk with him about the game. I later downloaded the game on my iPad and was immediately hooked on the game just like he was. Next time I saw him, I let him know how much I enjoyed the game as well and we kind of further connected. It began with us just having chats or talking after Sunday service.

I don't recall exactly how it happened, but somehow, he had given me his phone number. We eventually ended up talking on the phone and an interest was sparked. I even did some work for him. I designed his business cards and certificates for a training program he taught. During this process, he was drawn to my work ethic and ambition. He complained that his wife lacked ambition and that she was content just going to work on her job, which bothered him. This is what drew us close, our ambition and wanting more out of life than just working a job. We both desired to be entrepreneurs. We talked more on the phone, text, and then it too evolved into cyber-sex, just as I had with the other guy.

With both of those guys, it got to the point that it did as a result of seeds sown during our phone conversations. Our conversations were always filled with sexual comments, suggestions, information, or shared thoughts. So, I was juggling these 2 members when I had alone time apart from my husband. I did tell member #2 about member #1. My husband eventually found out about my cyber-indiscretions with member #2. Of course, he ran to tell the Pastor, who already knew because I told on myself. I even admitted to the Pastor that I'd shown them my private parts and had seen theirs via our conversations on the video app.

I was always telling on myself. That's how my husband found out; I told him. During an argument, after I found out about another indiscretion of my husband's, I argued that I had the opportunity to cheat, and I told him with whom, but I didn't cheat. I hadn't had sex with these men, at least not physically. Still, after he learned of my interaction with member #2 and another guy who I talked to, my husband put me through living Hell for three years. Mind you, with his infidelity, he actually had sex. I hadn't, but he still put me through Hell as if I had. He made me change my phone number, and I had to check in by calling him just about every 5 minutes and so forth. In fact...I told my husband one day, "If you keep accusing me of sleeping with someone, you will eventually live those words." He did not realize the potency of the new seeds he was constantly sowing into me.

Three years had passed. One year, my temp assignment that I was working on at the time ended abruptly and it kind of devastated me. The agency couldn't find me a new assignment right away. Since I now had a lot of free time on my hands, I told the Pastor that I would come back to work at the church with him. I had done so every time I was in between temp assignments but they were short periods. This time my unemployment lasted a lot longer than expected. Me doing this also freed up my evenings to be a wife at home, although I was living in Hell. I started working at the church during the week, several days a week. This time was different than the other times.

CHAPTER 3

The Pastor's Secretary

When you are in a position of authority, there's a certain standard that you must uphold and you should command others to uphold a standard towards you and your authoritative position. It should be an automatic response to respect those in authority and hold them to a high standard and accountable to righteousness, especially a man or woman of God who preaches and teaches the word of God. Even if the authoritative figure lowers their standard in how they interact with others, others should still respect them and their position. Thus, not putting them on your level, and not putting yourself in a place of familiarity with them.

The Pastor would often say, he had to be careful with how he interacted with the members of his congregation because he didn't want them to become familiar with him. However, his actions did not align with his statement. His actions showed differently, so it made it quite hard for the members not to slip into familiarity. He made personal calls to members, engaged in banter and chit chat with members after church, engaged in their personal business, invited people over to his home to hang out and hung out at members' homes as well as in public places, attended holiday and birthday celebrations with the members, and then had conversations with men and women that included him making jokes and comments of a sexual nature. I witnessed all of this or was a participant. Due to our close working relationship and how we casually interacted with one another, I can honestly say that I put myself at a place of familiarity with him. I tried not to, but it was quite hard to keep it at bay when he was extending the "friend" olive branch. The tides turned really quickly in terms of our working relationship and interactions with one another.

I didn't directly come on to him, and he didn't directly come on to me. The seed from the Pastor was sown when it all started with a subtle joke he made with a sexual undertone that I responded back with my own sexual undertone. I had taken the bait. One day we were talking in his office, and because it was a hot day, he started emulating the chorus to the song, *"Hot in Herre,"* by Nelly. I playfully joined in and sang the rest of the line from where he stopped. He paused for a moment, obviously caught off guard by my response. But he regained his composure, and replied, "Oh, so you really are cool!" The reason he said that is because I was really mean to everybody, including him. It didn't really matter that he was the Pastor. Bless the Lord, I am free from that now too, but then, I was just a mean, angry, bitter, Christian woman with an exceedingly bad and nasty attitude. That seemed to change in that instance and we started talking about getting some ice cream. Everybody knew how much he loved ice cream.

He said, "Do you like to lick it," referring to the ice cream, to which I responded, "I like to be licked." Then the playtime between us started and continued on for several years because the seed was planted, it had taken root, and was continuously being watered daily. I meditated on every seed that was sown. I meditated not just on the initial seed, but also having full-blown thoughts of it ending with us having sex, even though we had not even gotten that close.

The sexual comments and innuendos between the two of us continued, then moved to sexual talks, then to suggestive looks and gestures, and then to touching. It seemed that he got into my heart really quickly. Or should I say, lust rose up in me quickly and deeply. I was already at a tremendously vulnerable place. As a result, I opened myself up to other individuals who also took advantage of my vulnerability and brokenness of which they knew about because of conversations we had. But, I can also say that I did the same with member #1. He too was vulnerable, and in his vulnerability, he found it difficult to tell me no.

My husband and I had been having much trouble in our marriage because of my previous actions with the member he found out about. The Pastor knew this information as well. What do you think a Pastor should do when he knows that members in his congregation are having trouble in their marriages that are leading to their inappropriate interactions with other members? You would think the correct response would be to rebuke, reprimand, and correct those members. And he himself would cut off his interactions with the female party, especially after she is the one who confessed to what was going on. Yeah, no, that's not what happened at all.

I told him about my interactions with the other guys. I told him we talked, texted, and would "show ourselves" to each other over video chat. He told me to cut it off with them, and I did to some degree, or so he thought. He was disappointed in me and insisted that I end the interactions, but I didn't and I later got caught by my husband when he found out that I sent pictures, although I was fully clothed in them, to member #2.

As for me, the new attention was immensely welcomed, especially to think that the Pastor would have any interest or attraction to me. Because even during that time, although I was flirty, I still had extremely low self-esteem and a fear of rejection. Even my husband would complain that I was too flirtatious around men, which I denied because I couldn't see it. I called it being friendly. However, since I had come from a past of being particularly seductive because I was a former stripper, I could exude confidence when I wanted to.

At that time, the Pastor did not have this information concerning me. He learned of it during our many "pillow talks," so to speak, when we would talk in the office. He even coined a nickname for me, calling me "Sally the Seducer." He also would joke with the young guys around the church telling them not to look into my eyes because if they do, they would get hooked. This actually was true… but they didn't listen, and did get hooked. Over time, they saw that I was cool, playful, and flirty, and they engaged me in such talks and conversations. You could say that I was really enjoying the attention again, seeing as though I'd been 12 years removed from the clubs. But I knew my limits. I would only play with them around church —absolutely nothing further. Since I wasn't really talking to the other two members much anymore, the Pastor had all my attention.

When the Pastor didn't make me "sit down" from my church responsibilities after I was caught "behaving inappropriately," my husband actually left the church. I stayed although my husband was trying to make me leave. At this point I couldn't leave because of the new relationship I now had with the Pastor. My indiscretions with the other members did put a slight damper on our relationship, but it also opened the door for all the focus and attention to be on him. I will go out on a limb and say that his learning about my interactions with the other members was probably a seed sown into him and trigged his curiosity.

After my husband left, he kept really close reigns on me. Really close. My husband wasn't there to watch either, and he made sure that he knew I wouldn't leave because my husband had left. He would say something like, my husband left because he was offended and therefore, he was out of the will of God and if I left, I would be out of the will of God too. In spite of all the other behavior, I believed that I didn't want to be out of the will of God, so I endured the torment that ensued at home because I refused to leave the church. But one reason I wouldn't leave is because after he left, my husband wasn't even going to church, and this went on for a full 6 months. Besides, why should I follow him and leave to only stay home. Hmmm. Besides, I was enjoying my new interactions with the Pastor and didn't want to lose that.

After Sunday services, there were some people who often left immediately after, and there were many others, especially leadership who stayed for hours after, talking and fellowshipping with one another. Oftentimes the church would have sporadic events after service where there were refreshments served. One day after one of those events, I happened to be engaged in conversation with member #2. The Pastor noticed this. When I finished conversing and went over to the Pastor, he grabbed me, holding onto me, pulled me in closely and said in my ear, "You cheating on me." I laughed at first, but when I saw he was serious, I responded with, "No." He said, "You better not be," then he let me go and walked away. That action and statement completely caught me off guard and I definitely knew that his attention was on me.

One day I came to work wearing a sundress. It was a purple and white halter sundress I had bought it months prior and had never worn it. It was summertime and generally hot. In the summertime, I didn't wear underwear because I did not like to sweat in my private area. At some point in our conversation that day, I mentioned this to him. I said it to see how he would respond. It kind of lit a spark in our day because we were extremely flirty and playful with one another that day. He made the suggestion for me to lay on the couch that was in his office, I did so. He came over to me and laid on top of me. He then got up to close the office door while saying, "If you raise your dress up, then I know you want me." I started to raise it but I was hesitant and extremely nervous. This was the Pastor after all, how could I be doing something like this with him. Then again, I wanted him to be the one to raise up my dress, that would signify to me that he wanted me. I teased as if I was going to raise it but actually didn't, and he responded, "You must don't want me," as he came back to lie on top of me after closing the door. It wasn't that. By this time, I really wanted him. I was really nervous about it and so was he, I could tell, so we didn't go any further that day. Later, as we were leaving for the day, he stated that he was grateful that I didn't raise my dress. "If I went down that rabbit hole, I probably wouldn't be able to get out," he said.

From that moment on, when I wore dresses or skirts to church on Sunday's, he made it a point to ask me if I was wearing any underwear. Oftentimes, he awaited my response, other times, he would tell me that he could tell when I wasn't wearing any, or he would feel to see for himself *behind closed doors.*

After that day, we pulled back from one another to evaluate what happened. I was feeling really convicted. We both knew it wasn't right. However, at that point we were in too deep, at least I thought so, and our pull towards one another was very strong and we just couldn't stay away. I felt strongly about him in my heart. Days later, one evening we talked about things, I expressed what I was feeling and he sent me some information about non-sexual soul ties while we were on the phone. *Apparently*, he had already researched it and was feeling something himself.

More things began to happen. We were sneaking around, and making sexual eye contact even when others were around, trying to avoid getting caught. Behind closed doors, there was more touching, petting, sexual talk and the like. More communication, not only at the office, but outside of the office. Our personal phone calls increased. I didn't have an iPhone like he did. Since we couldn't Face-Time, I persuaded him to download the app I had on my phone so that we could video chat. Of course we had to secretly do this when we were home with our spouses, but we would have our video chats to "see one another." I was mostly home alone, so he would sneak down to his basement to talk to me.

Later, he had gotten an iPad and because they were the new "in thing," I wanted one so badly. I pleaded with him to get me one through the church for "work purposes," and I even discussed the idea with his wife. But, I also wanted it for the FaceTime and messaging capabilities. Apparently, he and his wife had discussed it amongst themselves to get me one for Christmas. At some point, he mentioned it to my husband, but my husband was not going to let that happen. He was already having suspicions that something was going on with the Pastor and I during this tenure of my working at the church. So that Christmas, my husband bought me an iPad. I was so thankful and excited. This was the icing on the cake to take our out-of-office conversations to a whole other level. I now had the ability to Message and FaceTime the Pastor.

There were many days while working at the church that we hardly got any work done. We spent a lot of time talking and flirting and pretty much being all over one another. Except for Thursdays. That was the day he worked on his Sunday's sermon so he was strictly off limits on that day, including no phone calls. For the majority of the day, he stayed in his office with the door closed and I stayed in mine. If he needed me, he would call me to come to his office, otherwise, we kept it serious on Thursdays...most times.

He's told this particular story a couple of times during his sermon where he ran into a pothole leaving the church office one day because it was dark out. He was late going to pick up his daughter. The reason why he was running late that is never mentioned in the sermon, of course, is because after we were planning to leave, we spent more time in the parking lot, talking with one another. We really had great conversations, especially when our conversations were flirty, and sexual in nature so it made it all the more difficult for us to part, especially for me. I made him late getting home many nights and he would always joke, "You are going to get me in trouble," referring to his wife. I no longer cared. When we would leave, we would call one another after getting into our cars and talked until he got home because he lived closer to the church than I did. And I would text him when I got home. Eventually, most evenings, we would have message conversations on our iPads.

We even had our "couple moments," so-to-speak where things were not always good. We got into arguments or truly heated disagreements. One time, things got heated between us in front of his wife and a couple of other members. This particular day of work, we were joined by other people who were there for a special meeting. His wife, a board member, the member/minister who cleaned the church, and my daughter were there with us. They were gathered in the bookstore talking. I came in and joined them, excited to show the Pastor the finished product of a new CD label I'd been working on. I made several variations for him to choose his favorite. The Pastor, his wife, and the other people there looked them over. When he made a decision on the one he liked, I disagreed with his decision. Anger quickly arose in him. He slammed his hand down so hard on the bookcase they were standing near and yelled loudly, "I'm the Pastor!" That reaction shocked everyone. His hand slam was so hard; it broke the edge piece off the wooden bookcase.

I stormed out the bookstore and went into my office and closed the door. My daughter was sitting in there and she heard the commotion. I was shaken up, but I went back to work. My daughter didn't like the fact of me continuing to stay there and work after his reaction and commented that we should leave. I told her that I was ok. My feelings for him wouldn't let me leave. Once the others left, including his wife, he called me into his office. First he expressed how he felt about my disagreeing with him in front of others and called it disrespect to him as a Pastor. I apologized. He proceeded to express himself emotionally and we both ended up crying together. That was our last public display of disagreement.

I later found out, after I'd left the church, that the board member who was there that day discerned during that outburst there had to be something inappropriate going on between myself and the Pastor. His discernment was correct. He confronted the Pastor with his concerns and suggested he change our working relationship. Because that didn't happen, that member decided to leave the ministry.

CHAPTER 4

Behind Closed Doors

The calling of a Pastor is to be a Shepherd over God's people. The Pastor's role is to provide spiritual leadership to the members of the congregation, prepare sermons with interpretation of scripture, preach or teach, and conduct worship services. They should provide care and counsel to the members and assist them in crisis situations. Pastors also officiate special services such as weddings, baptisms, and funerals. They also collaborate with other church leaders for the day-to-day operations of the ministry[3]. The primary roles of the Pastor are spiritual in nature, as it pertains to their church responsibilities. A Pastor's role generally steps out of the spiritual nature when they are leading their family in the home; while it is natural, the family is still governed by spiritual principles. Furthermore, when a Pastor prepares and ministers the Word of God, messages of faith to bring about change in the lives of the congregants, there is an expectation that they would not have any behavior contrary to what they have preached or displayed in the pulpit.

The role of members in the congregation is to respect the calling and duties of the Pastor and not try to take it outside of the confines of the role, especially between Pastor and member of the opposite sex. When the members are in leadership roles and positions within the ministry, they too take on a higher behavioral standard to reflect not only the nature of Christ, but also of the Pastor under whom they serve. Members in leadership are not only representatives of Christ but representatives of their leaders, especially the Pastor.

When the Pastor preached, his messages were of faith that were helpful to build up spiritually to those who listened to what was being taught. After the preaching was over, the talk and actions changed. Not only the talk of the Pastor, but mine and other members and leaders included. Judging my own conversation and actions and those of others, listening in on conversations I overheard, I would often wonder if any of us paid attention to what we just heard during service. We had even participated in praise & worship, with our hands uplifted, shouting out praises unto God, and crying in our seats or at the altar in response to God's presence. Still, it seemed that almost immediately after the service was over, everything that happened during it was gone, just like a vapor. Ephesians 4:29-30, *"Do not let any unwholesome talk come out of your mouths, but only what is helpful for building others up according to their needs, that it may benefit those who listen. And do not grieve the Holy Spirit of God, with whom you were sealed for the day of redemption."*

Lust of the eyes and lust in the eyes is a powerful vice. You can often tell what people are thinking or how they feel about someone based on the way they look at them. I am guilty of my face telling on me. My facial expressions give me away long before my mouth or actions could speak. Body language speaks just as strongly as words. And when there's lust between two people, the body language is much stronger. Job said in chapter 31 verse 1, *"I made a covenant with my eyes not to look lustfully at a young woman."* Jesus said in Matthew 5:28, *"But I tell you that anyone who looks at a woman lustfully has already committed adultery with her in his heart.*" The eyes — what they focus on and how they focus on something or someone — controls how the body and soul will react. Lust for a person does not start with actions, but it starts with looking with the eyes.

I became an appeasement after he labored in the pulpit delivering the message, greeting/counseling the members, and socializing after services. It was my look, my touch, hug, reassurance that he looked for on Sundays and sometimes Wednesdays behind the closed doors of his office. I often wondered if his armor bearer on the other side of the door ever knew or wondered what was going on when we were inside the office alone. In a way I felt like he did, especially at some point in time, when he himself flirted with me and tried to have subtle talks with me in the same manner that the Pastor did.

The Pastor continued to bait me in for his own desires and egotistical emotions to make himself feel better and without knowing or realizing what it was doing to me, mentally and emotionally. On a continual basis, he was sowing the seeds of lust into me but not willing to follow-through on fulfilling them. I got strongly attached mentally, emotionally, and physically. I also made my own advances towards him that weren't denied, so you can say that I baited him as well. However, I believe mine were more emotional than for ego; not to see if "I still had it," which is more of the attitude he seemed to have. He had been married for over 30 years, so having women attracted to him was an appeasement. I couldn't stay away. I wanted to be around him all the time, talk to him all the time, touch him all the time, and feel his touch. He fed off of my needs, but I could tell that he needed it from me too. It was rarely spoken but widely displayed in actions and interactions. As the saying goes, "Actions speak louder than words," and many of his actions towards me and with me were very loud.

It took lots of praying, deliverance, and counseling for me to finally break free of the stronghold of the soul-tie from him.

By now, you may still be wondering what happened behind closed doors for me as The Pastor's Secretary, so let me continue to talk about *what really happened behind closed doors* in my interactions with the Pastor.

On multiple occasions I got asked the question, "Your tubes are tied, right?"

"Yes," I would reply.

"So you can't get pregnant," I would be asked.

"Nope, I can't," I would respond.

Why was I being asked this question??? Did it mean you're intending to have sex with me without using a condom? Or if we just happened to have sex, there are no condoms available, let's be sure that there is no possibility of me getting pregnant?

Somehow, in one of our sexual conversations it came up that I enjoyed oral sex. As a result, on an ongoing basis — in person, on the phone, FaceTime, whatever— he would always move his tongue in a licking gesture, as if to be licking me. He knew that aroused me. When he did it in person, sometimes I would rush off to the restroom to wipe away the wetness that it caused between my legs. He would even put two fingers up to his mouth and put his tongue through as a gesture. He enjoyed seeing me squirm in my seat when he did this. When we would talk on the phone and the conversation would take a sexual turn, he would say, "Guess what I'm doing," referring to him licking out his tongue. He knew exactly how that was affecting me, even through my imagination because then he would say, "Let me hang up and let you go to the restroom." That's how strong it was.

I recall a time when I had to FaceTime him late one night to approve a graphic I had been working on. While on FaceTime, he went to show his wife the graphic for her okay. Once she gave her ok, he left the area where she was, went and laid back on his bed and started doing the licking gesture. I wish I could say that the calls were the full extent of our involvement, but as you continue to read, you will see that those seeds only led to bolder ventures.

There was this one time, it was one Wednesday, he needed my help with his computer while preparing for bible study that day. I went into his office to show him what to do, so I leaned over the computer from the side of his chair. He pulled me over in front of him so that I could be in directly in front of the computer, and then I sat in his lap. While I still worked on his computer, I was being playful and started grinding on him. But then his manhood quickly rose, and he eventually jumped up and told me to take the seat. He didn't get up soon enough, however, because pre-ejaculation had happened and it showed on the medium stone washed jeans he was wearing that day. His white Polo shirt wasn't long enough to cover the spot, and he was frantic and hoped that it would dry up before the others began to arrive at the church.

On another day, there was a community meeting for local area Pastors held at the church. We worked hard preparing for it. I pulled into the parking lot of the church the morning of the meeting, and my heart sank when I saw his wife's SUV parked in her spot. I just knew that day I was not going to get any attention from him... or so I thought. He was really professional during the meeting. After the meeting was over, everyone left, including his wife. I didn't know how to approach him, especially since he was in Pastor mode, as there were times, when he was in Pastor mode, he was off limits. I thought that was the case for that day.

Everyone was gone and I joined him in his office to debrief on the meeting and it was back to normal for us. I was a little shocked, but relieved. We had our normal flirtatious conversations and touching. When we got hungry, we both decided to get something from a popular burger restaurant in our area. I placed a telephone order, and we drove separate cars to pick up the food. He gave me his credit card and I went in to pay and get our food. When I came out of the restaurant, I got in his car on the passenger side to give him his food. We flirty chatted for a minute, but he was nervous that we'd be seen, so I quickly got out and went back to my car and we talked to one another through the car windows.

Now there was one day that was a really good one. I was feeling really frisky. Actually at this point in our relationship, I was extremely frisky whenever I was around him. I had a very important project that I was working on, so I wasn't working in my office that day, but was working on a computer in the sound room of the church. Whenever I had to work on a large project, I had to use that Mac computer because the old computer I had in my office did not have the capacity to handle large graphic projects using Photoshop. I was designing a new banner for outdoor advertisement.

He was working in his office. I called him to come take a look at the progress of the banner that I was working on. He came into the sound room, leaned over really close to me like he normally did, being his usual playful self. He gave his feedback and we flirted with one another for a few moments as we always did. That was our normal type of conversation. Instead of going back to his office, he sat in a vacant chair at the table. I got up and went to where he was seated. I turned his chair towards me and straddled him. It caught him off guard, and I could tell it made him a bit nervous, but he didn't stop me, not initially. After a few moments, he pushed me away, but then put his hands around my butt, and he pulled me back towards him. We grinded for a bit with him pushing me away and pulling me back towards him several more times until he thought it was best we quit.

He nervously retreated back to his office, I stayed where I was to continue working on the project. Later, I called him back to take a look at the banner again to see the progress I had made, and although flustered, he was still in his playful mood. He did a gesture he'd done several times before. He put his hand on the back of my head, pulling my face towards his crotch, and I playfully acted like I was pleasuring him until he stopped me saying "Girl, you are crazy."

CHAPTER 5

Valentine's Day

The more a seed gets watered, the more it grows. If you plant seeds of a sexual nature and continue to water them with words, actions, and meditating on sexual content, the root of the seed is going to run deep and begin to grow until its harvest time. Any type of sexual seeds sown have the potential to create a soul-tie. A soul-tie is an emotional bond that connects you to someone else. You become bound to that person through your soul. A soul tie is formed through relationships and mainly through physical intimacy. Intimacy is not just sexual. It is defined as *close familiarity or friendship; closeness. A private cozy atmosphere, an intimate act, especially intercourse. An intimate remark.* Intimacy is the initiating factor to a soul tie being formed. The way you are bound to another person is emotional— in your thoughts and your feelings— and generally that person has a dominant place within you.

Soul ties through sexual and non-sexual intimacy can both have the same powerful effects on people. Because of the major prominent effect soul ties have on people and how it affects their lives, many ministers have done extensive research and teachings on soul ties. In a teaching, *Break-*

ing Soul Ties[1], Terri Savelle-Foy states, when you spend an excessive amount of time thinking about a person or meditating on them and your interactions with them, you have a soul-tie. When you find yourself constantly wanting or needing to be around that person and you can't stand to see others occupying their time or space, you have a soul-tie. A soul-tie is very powerful and it is fed or fielded by how you interact with one another. Even after you have moved on past the relationship, if you find that person dominates your thoughts and you even meditate on the memories of your interactions together, you are in a soul-tie, and it will need to be broken.

I found a more in-depth look at soul ties on Kris Vallatton's blog, *7 Signs of an Unhealthy Soul Tie[2].* In each description, I could clearly see my own situation proved that I was dealing with my own soul ties.

1. *You are in a physically, and/or emotionally, and/or spiritually abusive relationship, but you "feel" so attached to them that you refuse to cut off the connection and set boundaries with them.*

The fact that he was my Pastor speaks volumes that boundaries should have been set so that I/we would not get in a position of being emotionally attached to one another. We were in an emotionally charged relationship which we knew was wrong, but we refused to cut off our connection with one another or set specified boundaries that would not include close contact or interactions.

2. *You have left a relationship (maybe long ago), but you think about the other person obsessively (you can't get them out of your mind).*

I know for me, when I could tell the relationship was over, I still couldn't get him out of my mind. Whenever I went to church and would not receive any attention from him, not even a hello, it would drive me crazy. And I hated to see him talking to and interacting with other women who I felt he was interested in, especially based on flirtatious conversations I heard and interactions I witnessed him having with them.

3. Whenever you do anything - make a decision, have a conversation with someone, etc., you "feel" like this person is with you or watching you.

I was so loyal to the Pastor, that I sought his approval for my activities with my own husband. Whenever there was something my husband wanted to do with me or if he wanted to take me on a date or trip, I would tell the Pastor first before I agreed to do it. He would often object or state his displeasure in the activity/activities my husband and I were planning to partake in, especially secular concerts, which my husband loved to go to, even if he found out after the fact. He was especially displeased with the activities that caused us to be absent from church, such as vacations or out of town trips, but I had to do them anyway.

4. When you have sex with someone else (your husband or wife), you can hardly keep yourself from visualizing the person you have a soul tie with.

Once while having sex with my husband, especially when my husband was pleasuring me orally, I imagined it was the Pastor. Mainly because we often had conversations about oral sex and the gesture he often made when we were together to get me aroused.

5. You take on the negative traits of the person that your soul is tied to and carry their offenses whether or not you actually agree with them.

I was always at his defense. I would always defend him against anyone speaking negatively about him, including my family or my husband's, and I would always tell him what other people have said about him or his wife. He taught us that it's our duty to show loyalty to our Pastor by not letting anyone talk about them, and that we, the members, should not talk about them either. I had to cut associations with people who spoke against the Pastor, and I lost some really close relationships because of this.

6. You defend your right to stay in a relationship with the person that your soul is tied to, even though it is negatively affecting or even destroying the important relationships in your life (hus-

band, wife, kids, leaders, etc.).

When I knew my feelings for him were growing and my husband began to take notice and complain about me "working too much," or "talking to the Pastor too much," when we were working on church projects, I defended my right to maintain my position through the work I did for the Pastor and the ministry to disguise my true feelings. Even when the Pastor (by way of orders from his wife) secretly shifted me out of my role, he found a way to keep me on the Leadership team until I was eventually phased out completely.

7. *You have simultaneous experiences and/or "moods" as the person your soul is tied to. This can even include sickness, accidents, addictions, etc.*

The Pastor was very moody at times and I found myself joining him in his moodiness when I was around him. He was also very temperamental. That was one thing we had in common, and oftentimes, our tempers flared up against one another, and were even quite explosive. We would cry together when we upset one another, and then kiss & make-up (so to speak).

The one day I must say was the most fun, friskiest but turned riskiest day for us was on Valentine's Day one year. It was still pretty cold out, so that day I wore a gray, turtle neck, A-line sweater dress, and some boots. It wasn't fitted at all. Nope, I didn't wear any panties, it was Valentine's Day! On my way to the office, I stopped by a store and bought a card and some candy for him. It was just a small token of my love. No, he didn't buy me anything. We did have our usual lunch that day, but he always bought our lunch every day, unless he brought leftovers from home. Occasionally, he would buy us breakfast on the way to work, or some days I would. I wasn't getting paid, but he made sure that I wasn't without money. He would give me gas money and pocket change.

Back to Valentine's Day. I had been having issues with my office desk and had previously asked him to fix it several times. Maybe he considered this a Valentine's Day gift to me, and he decided to get it taken care of. He assessed the issue, got his tools, and came into my office to fix the desk. He got on the floor under the desk lying completely on his back. After a few minutes of him being under there, being my new-normal playful self, I got out of my chair, got down and straddled him while he was on the floor. I was playfully gyrating on him and acting like I was dancing like back in my days as a stripper. He was like "Girl, quit playing, you're so silly." But I didn't stop. I stayed, and he didn't stop me either. We stayed in that position until he got done fixing my desk. He was tripping on me for being so bold, but it also ignited the lust in him. He kept coming back into my office and would get really close up to me. The one thing I can say is although we are bold enough to talk sexually to one another, and touch each other, neither one of us was bold enough to make the first move in kissing or sex.

Later that day, we ended up having a visitor. It was my husband. He was working his part-time job that day. He and his partner were in the area working and they stopped by. No, he didn't bring me a Valentine's gift either. My husband was walking around the church, giving his partner a tour, and the Pastor joined them in conversation. You would think guilt would be all over us because of the earlier events. Not so. As my husband was leaving, I walked them out and I locked the door behind them…supposedly. I went back into his office this time and someway, somehow I ended up on his couch, he came over, and laid on top of me. This happened right after my husband left. Next thing you know, we heard voices and it was my husband coming down the hall. He jumped up off of me so quickly. Our hearts pounding, I rushed out of the office to assess how he got back into the building. Apparently, I hadn't locked the door completely. After my husband left again, we both were a nervous wreck. He kept making me get up and go check the door to be sure it was locked before we picked up where we left off. Most days he kept the shades to his office windows closed or just slightly open. Following my husband's visit, he opened them so that we wouldn't be caught off guard by more surprise visitors.

Later that evening, I was supposed to go to my daughter's basketball game which was a long way away in another town, but neither of us wanted to leave one another's presence. I ended up leaving much later than I needed to and was extremely late to the game. My plan was to meet up with the father of another player and we were supposed to ride to the game together. This father and I had been talking to one another on the phone. At other games, my husband noticed how this father looked at me and interacted with me when he may have thought my husband wasn't looking. Naturally, this made my husband think we had something going on. When I walked in the gym, I took the first available seat I saw, which happened to be by this father and the father of another of my daughter's teammates.

I wasn't expecting my husband to be at the game because I thought he was still working. Well I was wrong, and my husband saw me from across them gym and came over to confront me, causing a scene. I got up and followed my husband as he stormed out of the gym. We were arguing in the lobby in front of people. My husband tore out of the school, leaving the game before it ended. I couldn't leave because I had to bring our daughter home. Of course, my first instinct was to call the Pastor and let him know what was going on. I even told him that me and the guy were supposed to ride to the game together, and he said it was a good thing that we didn't since my husband was there. I actually had been secretly talking to him but that's it. My husband and I were already having major issues in our marriage, and after that scene, he threatened to commit suicide. The Pastor had to try to keep me calm so that I could bring peace to my household that evening.

CHAPTER 6

Smoothie

For men and women of God who are the leaders of members of their congregation, there are just some areas of conversations that should be off limits. Members should also be mindful of the types of conversations they are having with their leaders. The leader already has to deal with many factors because of their position. They have to be equipped to teach the word of God, and hear the problems of their members to give counsel. Therefore, members should have boundaries and avoid ungodly and unwholesome communication, especially within the confines of the ministry or on the grounds of the church. And ungodly and unwholesome communication should not take place between leaders and congregants.

But there were no more boundaries. At this point, the level of authoritative respect no longer existed. I still used the title "Pastor" verbally, but in my mind, I would refer to him by his first name and felt like I was at the place that I could call him that. I was not told I could and I never asked. Although one time, we went to a craft store together to look for something, and he was all over the place, which frustrated me. He was quickly going up and down every aisle like a kid with ADHD. He noticed my frustration in trying to keep up with him. Laughing, he said, "How does it feel to shop with_?" and he said his first and last name. I responded that it was crazy. I wondered if he was like that all the time. I experienced glimpses of it while working with him at the church, but this was a whole new aspect.

As a matter of fact, I was very uncomfortable with him that day because it was a few days later after our first encounter on the couch, and I was trying to keep my feelings at bay and my hands to myself. The awkward ride to and from the craft store only increased my discomfort. He noticed a change in my demeanor and I told him that I was trying to exercise self-control. Especially since we both repented for our inappropriate interactions with one another and I didn't want to repeat it. I don't think he liked my self-controlled behavior too much because he made a couple of comments about it. I think I'd already disappointed God by laying inappropriately on the couch with the Pastor, I didn't want to get myself into deeper trouble with God.

Why didn't I ask if I could call him by name? I guess it was because I didn't want to do and/or say anything that would cause a disruption in our relationship. After having a strong connection and the place I was at with him, I feared being rejected by him if I asked to call him by name and not title, and I did not want that to happen. I just made up my own pet name for him, and I called him "Mr. Pastor." At some point later, I experienced rejection from him for about 3 weeks, and it was extremely painful to go through. I concluded that it would be best to stick with calling him "Mr. Pastor" rather than endure the torture of not having his attention or having him not talk to me for any period of time.

Our temporary separation was a result of me verbally confessing my love for him to one of his ministerial leaders. One day after an event, the three of us were sitting at a round table in the fellowship cafe area talking. During the conversation, I made the statement to the minister that I had strong feelings for someone. I didn't say any names and didn't think I gave any indication as to who I was referring to. The Pastor gave me a piercing stare at that moment but then later, I didn't hear from him and he would not take my calls and he avoided me at church. I was confused and didn't understand what happened. When he finally started to talk to me again, he said he was mad at me for what I said to the minister who had to have known who I was referring to. I didn't think he did. However, I was terribly, mentally and emotionally tormented during that time he kept me at bay.

When we were talking again, our inappropriate conversations seemed to begin without prompting. One day he asked, "When you shave your private area, do you just shave the hair low or shave all the hair off? I responded, "I shave the hair off completely, especially in the summer. I don't like to smell when I sweat." So I was smooth in that area. He then shared with me that his wife used his clippers to shave. That's about the only time he ever shared anything personal about her. But from that day forward, he ended any text message, IM, or email with a picture of a smoothie. That picture was indication that what was said during that conversation stuck with him.

For a Pastor to ask a married female congregant, especially his Secretary, how she shaves her vagina is out of order and for the woman to give a response to the question is equally out of order. The two should not have been in such a position to where that question would be asked. Where was the standard of morality and righteousness amongst the two? Who was supposed to raise or keep the standard? We obviously had gotten past the point of a professional working relationship. Our relationship was now casual and more intimate.

In his office, he would always sneak a rub or touch, even when his wife or other leaders were in there and "we were working" on something that required me to be near him at his desk. I would be devious too, standing closely so that our legs or bodies touched in some way. Other times he would sneakily touch my leg with his hands under the desk. This was kind of like fun and games for us. I must say, the sexual attraction was strong.

I remember one Sunday when I came to church devastated. I had just found out a few days' prior that my husband had given me a sexually transmitted infection. After service, the Pastor was in his office, and I found my way in there, as usual. But this time, I was crying and he hugged me close and tight. I told him what happened. He said to me, "Is this what it had to take to get you in my arms?" That was our most intimate embrace. I knew then that his feelings for me matched mine for him.

When it came to a point when we weren't spending too much time together at the office because I was working, we were talking more and more on the phone. Since I still worked on many projects for the Pastor, he would call me to talk about those projects or to give me an assignment to work on. Some of our conversations would be about church work. Other conversations would consist of me complaining about my husband. We had some good conversations though. Some were about general topics, and oftentimes, we would get in a little talk about the Word. I can say that when we had conversations about the word of God, he was very passionate. At the same time, many of our conversations were flirtatious. We simply had great camaraderie and liked talking to one another. We had grown closer and developed a strong bond. We had become really good friends.

There is one day in particular when I noticed the sexual attention had grown really strong. We were out at a restaurant celebrating another member's birthday. I had the responsibility of bringing the "birthday boy" to the restaurant since he lived near us. When we got to the restaurant, the Pastor and his wife were already there, along with everyone else who were guests at the celebration. I had chosen a seat directly across the table from the Pastor and his wife. Go figure! I had to be close to him all the time. But I ended up having to leave to go pick up my husband from work to come to the dinner because his car wasn't working. Our marriage was still pure HELL during this period. When we got back to the restaurant, I walked into the party area first thinking my husband would follow me to sit down and I went back to the seat where I was sitting previously. Although there was a seat next to me, my husband chose a seat at another table. I went over to him and asked why he didn't sit next to me and he responded sarcastically, "Go ahead and sit next to your other husband." I knew he didn't really mean what he had said, or did he? But I did go sit back in the seat where I had been sitting, near the Pastor. My daughter was already seated on the other side of me.

We had gotten our food, were eating, and almost simultaneously, the Pastor and I both looked up at one another at the same time, our eyes locked, and there was like an electricity that surged through my body. My feelings for him were strong and at this point, my husband no longer mattered. After the party was over, and everyone was leaving, he went to get his car, leaving his wife to wait for him to drive up and pick her up. My husband went to the restroom, so my daughter and I went to get my car, and was going to drive back to get him. The Pastor found me on the aisle where my car was parked and pulled up.

Since my daughter was in the car, we had a steal-away moment from our spouses. We had our usual chat. His eyes were burrowing into my soul and then he looked away, locking his eyes on my booty, as he usually did. I positioned myself outside of his car window in a manner so that he could see it anyway. When I knew I would be in his presence, I dressed in a way that would please him. I knew what he liked. He was a booty man, very much so. He enjoyed looking at it, touching it, and pulling it close to him. There were many times in the office when I would bend over and he would come up real close behind me, grabbing me around my waist and I would just nestle my booty into his crotch.

One time he had a minor surgery. I wanted to go visit him and take a get-well gift. We had talked on the phone during his recovery time at home, but I begged to see him. Finally, I was given permission to visit and I was excited at the opportunity. I knew peanut M&M's were his favorite, so I went to Target, purchased a large candy jar, bags of peanut M&M's, a get-well card, and balloons. I went to his house to deliver my gifts. His wife was home. We were out of the office during this time, so I left home to go visit. Later that evening I had a dinner to attend with the dance ministry, so I hung out at their house until that time. Of course when his wife's back was turned, we secretly flirted with one another and I made sure to move around the kitchen area that we were in and position myself so he could watch my booty.

He had a thing for booties. In fact, he watched mine for fun. At some point later, I figured out his type— light-skinned and big butt women— and I told him so. He laughed but didn't deny it. This made me reflect on the light-skinned, big butt women who either were or had been in our congregation and his interactions with them. I was neither light skinned, nor did I have a big butt; it was just average size. One time, he even mentioned what I revealed in one of his Sunday sermons. He said, "Fellas, when your type, light-skinned, big butt shows up, you have to exercise control." It was a message about having control over your flesh. He himself was weak in this area. He needed to listen to his own messages.

CHAPTER 7

Lust of the Eyes, Lust of the Flesh, Pride of Life

When you make a commitment to start living your life for Christ, you are taught and admonished to turn away from things and actions that do not please God: Sin! One of the main things that you're admonished to turn away from is sexual sin which the Bible calls fornication. 1 Thessalonians 4:3 says, *"To abstain from fornication,"* and 1 Corinthians 6:13 states, *"Now the body is not for fornication, but for the Lord; and the Lord for the body."* Fornication *is sexual intercourse between people not married to each other.*

Even though some teach that sin is sin and there is no big sin or small sin, you are mainly taught not to commit sexual sins because the Bible teaches that we should present our bodies as a living sacrifice, Holy and acceptable to God (Romans 12:1). The body should be a vessel that should be possessed in sanctification and honor (1 Thessalonians 4:4). Therefore, we should do all that we can to refrain from any sexual sin with the body.

For many who have lived a life engaged in sexual activity

prior to Christ, this is not generally an easy task, especially without deliverance, discipline, and renewing the mind to think differently pertaining to sex. For many, it can be a struggle when you're single, and it can still be a struggle even when you're married because marriage is not a cure for lust, especially when you are bound by it. 2 Corinthians 7:1-9 (NIV) states, *"It is good for a man not to have sexual relations with a woman. But since sexual immorality is occurring, each man should have sexual relations with his own wife, and each woman with her own husband. The husband should fulfill his marital duty to his wife, and likewise the wife to her husband. Do not deprive each other except perhaps by mutual consent and for a time, so that you may devote yourselves to prayer. Then come together again so that Satan will not tempt you because of your lack of self-control. Now to the unmarried and the widows I say: It is good for them to stay unmarried, as I do, but if they cannot control themselves, they should marry, for it is better to marry than to burn with passion."*

The problem that most often occurs in many marriages is that the wife is not always willingly giving herself to her husband in fulfilling her marital duty to him sexually, and you do have some men who don't fulfill their marital duty either. But the issue is that self-control is not exercised and thus, fornication and adultery are introduced. You can always tell when a man is not being fulfilled sexually at home and this was strongly evident with the three men I engaged with and with myself as well. Their wives were not upholding her marital duties and my husband was not either. There were times I asked my husband for sex and he flat out told me no. That is mainly the reason why we, me and these other men, attracted to one another, those kindred spirits within us and us not being completely sexually fulfilled at home; at least that is what they told me.

Being a married woman, I tried to keep the amount of masturbation I did really low. As a single Christian, I did it often and my rationalization was that I did it to keep myself abstinent. I know, crazy thinking. That's what being bound by the spirit of perversion and living filled with lust will have you thinking. However, that spirit had been awakened, although not initially by the Pastor. Remember the inappropriate actions with the 2 other church members I mentioned earlier? Well yea, by them. More to that story in the coming pages. But, I did feel guilty doing it even then, so I pulled back from it.

However, after my interactions with the Pastor, the desire to masturbate was awakened back in me all the more and I started back doing it. He had made me hornier than ever. I would do it alone just thinking about him. I would do it on the phone with him, even on FaceTime. It became a new-norm, again. There were times I would get off the phone with him and watch pornography to satisfy the desire that rose up in me. That was also something we talked about; both of us struggled with pornography, which we identified as something we got introduced to early in our childhood. For me it was around 9 years old when I found a stack of Playboy magazine's hidden in our bathroom. I struggled with this off and on from age 15-42.

Then there's the subject of pictures and videos. I remember the very first time I sent him a provocative photo. It was a late-night chat via IM. I sent it to him and he reprimanded me harshly. I felt so convicted. But then as we evolved in our relationship and he learned that I took pictures for my husband and kept them on my phone or iPad, he let his guard down pertaining to pictures. He knew I didn't have a password on my iPad so he would often ask to see my iPad. He would go to the photos icon and look at the pictures. After he started that, I started sending photos again. No reprimand. Then I started sending video snippets. No reprimand.

After a while, I put my photos and videos in a vault app on my iPad so my activity wouldn't be seen by my husband because I started taking photos specifically to share with the Pastor and the other guys. The Pastor would go in the vault to look (after asking me to unlock it of course).

I later found out that many, many years prior he had actually seen nude photos of me. My husband asked another male member of the church, who was an IT professional, to work on our home computer after it went down from a virus. The Pastor told me the member went through our files and saw the photos on the computer and showed them him and pleaded with me not to tell my husband. Therefore, his curiosity was already piqued.

Even at one point, the Pastor's son and I started having these types of interactions and I'd sent him videos as well. We didn't get in too deep in our interactions, and it just simply ended. "Like Father, like Son" was my thought as I would have my conversations and interactions with the son. I also learned that his son watched pornography because I was on the phone with him during the midst of his watching. He literally was just like his father. Oh yeah, and member #1 who I was behaving inappropriately with in the beginning, well he's the Pastor's nephew. That should tell you what spirit runs in that bloodline.

Since I was already sending photos and videos, on this one Veteran's Day holiday I was home from work and we were talking on the phone; that day was no different. I had made a new video and I was excited for him to see it. I'd worn a sexy, black lingerie one-piece lace bodysuit, fishnet stockings, and black thigh high boots. I recorded the video dancing on a stripper pole that I had in my home, to a new song by Ciara. His son and nephew had already seen the video.

He was home in his theater room in his basement; one of his usual talking spots for us whenever someone else was home. His daughter was home that day, unbeknownst to me, and she was working on his laptop. I also didn't know that she had synced his laptop, iPad and cell phone together. So, during our conversation, I told him that I was sending him something. Well, next thing you know he says, "Let me call you back." His daughter had come running down to him. He calls back and says she saw the video come through and told him to delete the message and not open it (but, too late). She told him that she was telling Mom. His wife called him. He called me back and says, "My wife is calling you and you better clean it up." What did I do? I lied.

When she called, I told her that I was having a conversation with two people at once on my iPad, the Pastor being one and I accidentally sent the video in the wrong message, and I didn't know I did so until after he called me about his daughter seeing it. She accepted the lie, and just asked me how I thought it made her daughter feel to see me, a married woman, send such a video to someone who is not my husband. I shrugged it off but told her that I know it makes me look bad. From that day forward I was getting really strong, bad looks from the family. I so badly wanted to tell them that it wasn't the first time he'd gotten a video.

For a few weeks, he kept himself at bay as well to let things die down. I took the fall as the bad guy. I suffered in silence for a tremendously long time letting them think I was the "only one" in the wrong. I believe it was after this incident that his wife no longer wanted me working for him.

This wasn't the first time I took the fall as the bad guy. In the beginning when member #2 and I were messing around, his wife found out because my husband made him tell her about the pictures, and I took the fall. I didn't reveal to them his interactions with me. Another silent suffering I had to endure while I was looked upon as the harlot. In none of these situations was I ever acting alone.

Then the Pastor tells me that his wife had gone through the cell phone bills and said that we talked on the phone too much and she didn't want him talking to me so much anymore. But, he had to appease the wife, obviously. Even so, it didn't cut him off from me. So, what did he do??? He stopped calling me from his cell phone. I had started working on a job, and he had my work number. Since I was no longer working at the church, he stopped going to the church to work and started working from home. Then he started calling me from the church office phone line at his house. Phone calls untraceable!

I had worked on this job for a little over 4 years, so I can say that this may have been a 2-3 year period. Also, his wife worked from home on Fridays. Fridays and Saturdays were usually torture for me because I didn't really get to talk to him much. I could only call him if it was absolutely about church work. That being said, while she was home on Fridays, if he ever left the house, he would just call me from the car. All was not lost. I still got some steal-away phone call moments from him. Except for the last year he did start back calling me from his cell phone after I was no longer involved in ministry. From this point, all of our phones calls were of personal nature. After the video incident, they secretly started filtering all the work that I did for the church to the daughter until I had nothing left to do. They did this sneakily without any communication to me. I was so mad at him for doing this, especially due to the nature of our relationship.

When I was working as the Pastor's assistant and running the marketing and publications area, I had no problem being in service because it was where I belonged. On the basis of our relationship, I wanted to be there more than ever before. However, as dynamics started to shift, and work was taken from me, I no longer had an eagerness to get to church, especially when my husband would miss a Sunday due to work. My husband was all about appearances, even when we weren't getting along, so we always had to be at church. Still, I was always expected to be in service every Wednesday and Sunday, and this was even after I was no longer in a leadership position. My attitude towards the Pastor and church had changed due to me no longer being in leadership, so I would arrive late. I would often complain that two of his other leaders frequently missed bible study, but I was "required" to be there. My complaints fell on deaf ears.

I clearly recall, one Sunday after service the Pastor came up to me, "Why were you late?" he said firmly, "I had to have the ushers give up your seat." I kind of had an attitude with him coming to me like that, but I responded, "That was ok, I was able to hear just fine from where I was." Of course he responded that was good, but that wasn't why he was concerned about me being late. I wasn't in my usual front row seat of the sanctuary. I realized it wasn't just the fact of me being in service, but I was also out of the place or position that I was secretly expected to be in. I didn't care at that point. Don't get me wrong. I enjoyed my seat on the front row. It showed a position of leadership and it also put me closer to him; something in me still wanted to admire him close up versus from a distance, even though my feelings for him had been interrupted. Years later, someone who was unaware of my relationship with the Pastor shared with me that the Pastor needed me in my seat to draw energy from me. He needed to see me.

He also put demands on me that he didn't have on his wife. One day, I questioned him about it. He said that he asks her and she declines. For example, he asks her if she wants to pray over the offering, and she responds, "No," with a gesture for him to do it, so he moves on. I told him he shouldn't give her a yes or no option; he should just tell her to come pray over the offering. That really bothered me how he didn't require her to be active in service, but he didn't make any changes in that area either. Then again, I didn't know what was going on behind closed doors of their relationship.

CHAPTER 8

God Knows and Sees All

When your actions are not of righteous behavior, you are allowed to continue in such behavior for a limited time before God snatches you out of it, especially after he's given you ample opportunity to correct yourself and stop the behavior. God gives us warning after warning by the Holy Spirit before He rebukes us, corrects us, or even exposes us in our sinful behavior.

Our all-knowing God knows exactly what's best for us, even when we don't know what's best for ourselves. And sometimes God's best plan for us may not be appealing to us. That is what happened to me. I had gotten so comfortable working with the Pastor at the church office that I no longer cared that I didn't have a job and was collecting unemployment. I was applying for jobs because I had to remain compliant with the unemployment agency's requirements. I had applied for jobs, and gone on interviews in hopes and anticipation of getting the job, but nothing, which was ok with me. After 9 months of the temp agency having absolutely no assignments for me, out of the blue, I got a phone call to go on an interview for a temp assignment. I went to the interview and afterwards, I prayed and told God that I did not want that assignment because I was not interested. On the flip side, when I interviewed for permanent employment positions I applied for, I would pray and ask God to bless me with the job. Either I liked the company, position, and/or the pay was really good. But I did not get any of those jobs I prayed for and that baffled me. With this particular position, neither the job description nor the pay was good, and I definitely was not interested in having it. But God. He knew what was best for me at the place I was in at the time.

I messed up and mentioned to a church member, the Praise & Worship Leader, that I interviewed at the company where she worked. It turned out that the interview was in her department, with her manager, and yep, you guessed it, she put in a "good word" for me. Ha! If only you knew the circumstances surrounding that. Well, let me just go ahead and say it. The member of the church who I "got caught" with, sending pictures and talking inappropriately to on my iPad, member #2, yeah him, was her husband and she knew about it. Although years had passed since all of that happened, her putting in a "good word" for me at that job was nobody BUT God. In fact, she had mentioned to her husband that I interviewed with her manager and that she made a favorable recommendation for me for the position. I called him to tell him that I'd gotten a position working with his wife, which he already knew. From that phone call, our communications convened again.

When they called me for the job, I wanted to decline the offer so badly, but I had to take it. I was one of the selected ones in a special program with the unemployment division who was required to meet weekly for job search programs and evaluations. One of the obligations was that you could not turn down any interview or job offer, or you would lose your unemployment benefits. I had to take the job. I was upset, disgusted, and became mad at God! I felt like this job was punishment for my indiscretions with the Pastor. The job was the lowest position in the department with a very low pay. I was making \$15/hour at 40 years old. Ugh! I was mad because why couldn't I have gotten "blessed" with one of the good jobs that I'd interviewed for and actually wanted.

However, the Pastor and I worked out our own plan. Since he would already be at the church, when I got off work, I would mad dash there "to do work," and we could keep seeing each other. Then the winter time came and I stopped driving my car to work and started catching the Park-n-Ride. The job was 45 minutes to an hour, in rush hour traffic, from my house. Sometimes I would go to the church after work, but other times I couldn't make it. And if it was too cold, he wouldn't go into the church office anyway and would just work from home. This restrained us a bit and limited us to only interacting on the phone and seeing each other on Sundays and Wednesdays, on which I arrived at the church as early as I could, especially trying to beat his wife there. But then, he and his wife started riding to church together on Wednesdays and this hurt my heart.

Although this started to limit our ability to be able to see one another and have our alone time, it didn't stop our communication. We talked even more now on the phone. A whole lot more...sometimes hours at a time while I was working. My manager never said anything about my extended personal telephone use. We talked so much, that I wouldn't even answer my own husband's phone calls while I was on the phone with him. We talked during my work hours, break times and during my lunch. When I was home, we would message each other because that was the only time I could do it, unless I was able to get to a Wi-Fi connection for my iPad so that we could FaceTime. We would message each other at night, especially after his wife went to bed. My husband was hardly ever home, so I had a whole lot of freedom.

There was this one time, one Saturday night, we stayed up very late until after 1:00am messaging one another even though he had to preach that Sunday morning. After he finished preaching and got back to his office, and me right along in there with him, he was really sleepy. He said it was all my fault that he was tired because I kept him up so late.

CHAPTER 9

Special Meeting

God knows exactly what lies ahead for every area and aspect of our lives. That is called omniscient - *knowing everything,* and God is truly all knowing. 1 Corinthians 10:13 clearly tells us with <u>every</u> temptation, God **will** make a way of escape for us that we will be able to handle it. The problem arises when we, oftentimes, don't like the escape that God has provided, or we can't see it as the escape. The scripture didn't tell us the way of escape would be subject to our liking, but what it did say is that it would be a way that we'll be able to bear it. Meaning, it wouldn't be hard or cause detriment to us.

Consequently, the issue with me was God gave me this job, albeit awful to me, but God was saving and protecting me from a place I didn't need to go and from causing someone else to go to a place they didn't need to be either. The reason why we find ourselves in problems is because once God has provided a way of escape, we interject ourselves back into that place He has brought us out of, or we just simply don't recognize the hand of God at work.

It was a Tuesday. The Pastor called me at work and said he wanted to have a meeting with me and another department head who was the leader of CD duplication. He wanted to meet with us to get us on one accord so that our departments worked together and not against one another. I was responsible for designing the CD jacket covers for all the sermon series, as the ministry was growing fast, so we had to keep up. He told me the meeting time was 6:00pm. Well, I got off work at 4:00pm, so I just went there straight from work to arrive early.

This day, I was dressed casually, but still sexy. I didn't know of the meeting before hand, so I had not dressed this way because I was going to see the Pastor. He was no longer working at the church, so he had to make a special trip to the church for this meeting as well. Besides, it was also the Praise & Worship team's rehearsal night. I wore an oversized, green patterned Michael Kors top and some form fitted black pants. When I arrived at the church, I saw that he was wearing a green Polo T-shirt and jeans. It was like we were in sync.

Of course, I was happy to see him and once I stepped into the doors of the church building, we lovingly embraced, as was our usual greeting. Generally, the maintenance guy cleaned the church on Tuesdays, but I don't believe he had come that day. The Pastor walked around the church doing inspections of the building. He normally did this from time to time and I followed him around as a sounding board as he complained about things that were out of order. Midcourse during his inspection, going from the front of the church to the back, he stopped to lean up against the windowsill, thinking and talking aloud. I let him think out loud for a few moments, then I walked up close to him and put my hands on his shoulders and started to rub them. He let me rub them for a little bit then he moved away. Apparently I was getting to him because I saw that he had gotten aroused. Before he could move away, I reached in to touch his growing manhood, but he blocked me.

There was a stack of chairs stacked against the wall and he moved over to them and leaned against them, his back facing me. I walked over to him, slid my hands under his shirt and started rubbing his back. I asked him to take his shirt off but he wouldn't. So, I just pushed it all the way up over his shoulders and gave him a nice, long back massage— rubbing, kneading, and caressing. Then I concluded the massage by putting soft gentle kisses up and down his back. When I concluded, his response was, "Wow, you are good with your hands and even better with your mouth."

Although it was still early, he was nervous about the time drawing closer to 6pm, but aroused, he moved away from the spot where he was planted during the massage. He went and sat down on the stage farther back in the area that we were in. I followed, then sat down next to him. I continued what I had started, massaging and kissing him up and down his back. After a few minutes, he got up, grabbed my hand, pulled me up and led me into a room near where we were seated; one that was used for floral decorations storage. He closed the door. He pulled me in really close to him and said, "You know if we do this, there's no turning back." Breathing heavily, I responded, "I know," ready for what I thought was about to happen, longing for the moment I'd been wanting for such a long time now. I wanted to finally feel him inside of me, as he often would tease me. We were beginning to pull down our pants, and he stopped. Once again, he couldn't go through with it. Disappointment…again! We regained our composure for the meeting. Of course, I had to go to the restroom and wipe away all the moisture that had gathered between my legs.

The time for the meeting came and I must say that we were both sexually charged, and there was an intensity in the room. While in the meeting, whenever the other lady would turn her head or get out of eye sight, he would make seductive and suggestive eye contact with me. We were daringly flirting with one another while in the presence of someone else.

Since the day that I was finally awaiting came but ended with me aroused and rejected, those seeds that were planted, rooted, and had been watered by all of our sexual-natured interactions, now needed to bring forth a harvest. *"When desire is activated, people don't want advice or wisdom, they want satisfaction,"* says Dr. Matthew Stevenson, III. This was so true for me at the place I was in at that time. The desire for other men outside of my husband had been activated in me so strongly, satisfaction had to be achieved.

CHAPTER 10

Harvest

Like I said in an earlier chapter, when seeds are sown, there will eventually be a harvest. The first seed was my husband's infidelity. The next seed was a series of inappropriate conversations and interactions with the two members. Then more seeds were inappropriate conversations and interactions with the Pastor. All of these seeds that were sown went through the full process of harvest as according to Mark 4:28. *First the blade*, me entertaining the advances and flirtations of other men, *then the ear*, my involvement in inappropriate behavior with church members and the Pastor, and finally *after that the full corn in the ear*, committing adultery.

When bad seeds are sown, the sower does not get to determine what harvest will come from those seeds. That is why we have to be careful and cognizant of the seeds we allow to be sown into us, but more importantly, the seeds we sow into others. As sowers, we are the responsible party for the harvest that comes as a result of the seeds we sow into others— good, bad, or ugly. The harvest that came as a result of seeds sown into me were not what I expected and nor what I would have planned for my life. If I can be frank, I'm quite ashamed of the end result of the seeds sown into me and my sowing into others through our interactions with one another.

I ask as you're reading the remainder of this chapter, please, please, please don't persecute me for what I'm about to share in this next segment. I have already beaten myself up enough over the years with conviction and condemnation. I do thank God for forgiving me of my wrong-doings and making me free in Jesus Christ.

When you are bound by the spirit of perversion, and lust is so strong in you, and lust-filled seeds are sown into you, it'll make you do crazy things. Without thoughts of your actions or consequences, and without thinking about who would get hurt in the process, all you think about is fulfilling your own fleshly desires. All I knew was that I was hurt, broken, and horny at this time in my life and needed those areas to be fulfilled and consoled. I was out there bad. I didn't care about anybody at that time. It was all about me and fulfilling the lust of my flesh. The book of Proverbs chapter 5 speaks about the Immoral Woman, but verse 6 (NLT) confirmed exactly where I was during this period, *"For she cares nothing about the path to life. She staggers down a crooked trail and doesn't realize it."* Like I said, I didn't care and I surely didn't realize that the direction in which I was going was leading me to self-destruction.

Please know that this is not just me telling my story about the unrighteous things I did, but it is also a teaching. My story has so many lessons to offer, and I hope that you are able to learn from my mistakes. You should learn that past behaviors that you do not have complete deliverance from can manifest later in life, even after salvation. You should learn that you can be affected by seeds that others sow into you and you sow into others. You should be aware that because you have a good relationship with a Pastor or leader of the opposite sex, boundaries should be set so that no inappropriate interactions occur. When you are married, there are certain behaviors you should not engage in or entertain from the opposite sex. Anything done without your spouse's knowledge, anything you have to sneak and do, is inappropriate and unrighteous behavior that should be avoided at all times.

Although I knew that my sneaking around with the members was wrong, because my first interactions were with the Pastor, I didn't think it was wrong because of who he was. At first, I would tell my husband about conversations with the Pastor and sometimes he would get upset. When I would relay my husband's response back to the Pastor, he would often say, "You tell him too much." His wife even told me this a few times when I confided in her about arguments or disagreements with my husband, especially when I would tell him about other men who tried to talk to me. Once I heard these statements from the both of them enough, I stopped telling my husband anything, especially about my conversations with the Pastor.

Even after my husband cheated on me, I'd always told myself that I would never cheat on or leave him for another man. But if I did, it would have to be with someone who had money rather than someone who I just loved because my husband had no money. We married for love. No one on the outside would ever know we didn't have money because of all the things he did for me or us that had monetary value. Little did they know that it was all at the sacrifice of not paying the mortgage, car note, or other household bills. We were living paycheck to paycheck, no savings, but looked liked we had it going on. I finally grew tired of living this way and wanted us to be better financial stewards, but no matter how much I protested, my husband did what he wanted when it came to money; he had a typical poverty mentality.

In the wake of constant loneliness, lack of quality time, and attention from my husband, my initial thoughts of not cheating (especially with anyone who didn't have money), quickly faded and whoever showed me any attention was a prospect. Truth be told, when you have insecurities, have been rejected, and are broken, you'll accept anyone who gives you just the right attention that will fill those deficits you have within you.

Many people are familiar with the intro from the popular R. Kelly song, "Bump n' Grind," talking about the mind saying no but the body saying yes. Although I knew it was wrong, I could not contain the lust of my flesh. And the bad thing is, I had sinned against my fellow brethren which the scripture, Luke 17:3, admonishes against. *Take heed to yourselves. If your brother sins against you, rebuke him; and if he repents, forgive him.* (Luke 17:3 NKJV).

Proverbs 2:16-19, NLT, warns us, *"Wisdom will save you from the immoral woman, from the seductive words of the promiscuous woman. She has abandoned her husband and ignores the covenant she made before God. Entering her house leads to death; it is the road to the grave. The man who visits her is doomed. He will never reach the paths of life.* As I read this scripture, I realized in my past, I was exactly the woman mentioned here; I was immoral, promiscuous, and leading men down the wrong road.

Although the Pastor and I were still having our moments, I now had added the others back into the equation. I knew they would be willing to fulfill the lustful desires that I had because we had already planted seeds within one another previously. Although I had previously cut off the relationships with the two church members before, since the Pastor was no longer a candidate for sex, I began my interactions with them again.

The only reason why I was able to entertain these other men is because they made time for me. Even though they had lives and wives, they made the time to spend with me, thus speaking my love language of quality time. This was something that I constantly begged my husband to give me, but he wouldn't comply. Even after he stopped working, quality time was still difficult to get from him. If I wanted time with my husband while he was home, I had to sit and watch television with him while he spent hours and hours on the couch doing so.

There was even another church member who entered into the mix, a married man, who was also a third cousin of my husband, on his mother's side of the family. He was very interested in me, for sex I'm sure. We talked occasionally via phone, text, and email. I wasn't interested nor was I attracted to him, so I kept things with him to a bare minimum. Although I'd sent provocative pictures to others, whenever he asked, I refused to send him any. Whenever he wanted to meet on FaceTime, I wouldn't. Something in me didn't trust him. My husband ended up finding some old emails of our communication after I cut off communication with this guy. He insisted that something went on and refused to believe me when I told him absolutely nothing happened, which was, ironically, the truth.

I started back talking to the first guy, the Pastor's nephew, after I had become one of the godmothers to their youngest son. I fell in love with that little boy from the moment he was born and first came to church. I had a love for both of their sons, so I often picked them up for weekend visits. Their father, who I playfully called my "Baby's Daddy," and I started interacting more again. Our attraction for one another was still there. We talked on the phone, text, and FaceTime. As a matter of fact, his wife was still checking his phone call history from his previous indiscretions, and she questioned why he talked to me so much. As not to arouse suspicion, he had me to download the TextMe app on my phone so we could talk and text without it being traced. We couldn't hold back, and we started having a sexual relationship with one another that went on for many months. We worked near each other, so we would often meet for quick chats and to see one another. We snuck around and met at different places. We had sex in his car, at my house, his house, parking lots, wherever.

He was even a member of the Praise & Worship team, of which my husband was a member of as well. He would sing on Sunday mornings after he and I had sexual encounters or cyber-sex interactions on a Saturday night. Just as bad, I was on the dance ministry team, and would dance on a Sunday morning after an encounter. With all the dance ministry training and teaching I'd acquired over the years, dancing while engaging in sin was dangerous, spiritually,. He also sang with a gospel band, and sometimes we would meet up to see one another either before or after his band rehearsals. I'd gone to their local shows as a supporting lover/groupie.

I wasn't his first affair. Therefore, he obviously was still bound by that spirit seeing as though he easily had an affair with me, even though he'd gone through hell with his wife from the first affair. I heard that he's admitted that he even slept with other women after me, although no one ever knew about me.

During our relationship, I was under heavy conviction of how I was secretly treating his wife. As a Godmother to their son, I was a part of the family. I loved them dearly and they loved me and my family. We were really a blended family. I was welcomed in their home and to family functions. I was extremely torn by my actions, but I was more fueled by the lust of my flesh. During this period, I never felt comfortable around my "Baby's Mama," as I affectionately called her because her baby, "son," was my baby too. When I was around her, masking who I really was at that time was a huge effort.

One instance in particular is when the Women's Ministry hosted a Pajama Party. His wife was a part of the committee, so she had to be at the church early. He called me, we talked, and he told me to come see him before I went to the church. I just expected I would go over there briefly; we would chat, flirt, kiss or what not. He had different thoughts than I did. What he did, I absolutely did not expect. When I stepped into the doorway of their home, we embraced, kissed a moment, he got aroused and next thing I knew, he turned me around, bent me over the stairs and pushed himself inside of me. After a couple of thrusts, I pushed him off. It was wrong and extremely risky because not only was I in their house, but I was also on my way to a Women's event at church, which his wife would be attending as well. I pushed down my dress and left.

I was late getting to the church because of my detoured rendezvous, but that's not the worst part. The worst part is that as soon as I walked in the door of the church, I was greeted by his wife, a big smile spread across her face at seeing me, and her arms opened for an embrace. I panicked on the inside. *What if she smelled her husband's scent on me?* I gave an extremely forced greeting and embrace and rushed away from her and made sure to stay away from her for the rest of the night. I went to the bathroom to wash up and change into the pajamas that my daughter had bought for me since I didn't go home after working late.

As I mentioned before, if you pay attention, God will always set you up or position you to come out of whatever sin you are in. We participated in several activities, then later that evening, the facilitator introduced a segment called "The Purge," that we ladies would be engaging in. The volunteers passed out some artificial leaves to every lady. She had an extra-large, clear glass vase set at the front of the room and gave the instructions. She would be calling out different topics, issues, subjects, behaviors, or challenges that people deal with in their lives. If anything pertained to us, we would go drop a leaf in the vase to declare and signify before God and others that we were ready for that area to be purged from our life.

I had already dropped in a few leaves for areas that pertained to me such as anger, bitterness, bad attitude—the simple things. But when she got to lust, sexual sin, fornication, and adultery, I didn't move. I remained in my seat, my heart beating nervously. I did so for a couple of reasons. One, I didn't want people to know that I was dealing with sexual sin; I was a married woman. Two, at that moment, I wasn't sure if I was ready or could give up what I was doing *behind closed doors*. However, God had given me the opportunity to release that. Now I know, had I taken that opportunity God's grace would have been present for my deliverance, I would not have traveled farther down the road that I was already on. It all reminds of the book by Tiffany L. Warren, *Farther Than I Meant To Go, Longer Than I Meant To Stay*, which is a very excellent read by the way. At the end of the Purge, she did say, if there was anything she called out and we didn't drop a leaf in and if we wanted to, we could come up and do so. I took that opportunity as I mumbled a "forgive me Father," even though I believed I'd already missed my window of deliverance because I hid behind my sin.

Another risky moment occurred when I was picking the boys up for a weekend visit. Their mother was not home. When I got there to pick them up, he'd just put them in the tub for a bath. As I sat on the couch to wait, he came over and got on the floor in front of me, pulling me down some from the couch while pulling my pants down at the same time. He then planted his face between my legs and went to work. After a few moments of that, he got up, pulling me up and pulled me downstairs to the basement to finish the work he started, bending me over for a moment of pleasure. This would be our last physical encounter. However, we continued to talk on the phone and have cyber-sex conversations. Including a specific time he went to Miami with his boys for his birthday and he called me up wanting me to send him a special birthday video, to which I obliged. I found a birthday song, dressed in a sexy, red lingerie outfit, and recorded a sexy chair dance in my bathroom at home. I saved the video, which I also sent to the Pastor for his birthday when it came months later.

Then, I also started back interacting with the other guy

who, as I mentioned, was the Praise & Worship leader's husband and he was head of church security. This interaction transpired after I started working with her. But at first, he and I only had telephone conversations. He too was still going through hard times with his wife because of our previous encounter and their own issues. Hence, he didn't really want me calling him from my cell phone. Initially, I would call him from my work phone when it dawned on him that his wife would recognize the number since we worked in the same place and because she was still checking the history of his phone calls. That being the case, I had him download the TextMe app on his phone so we could interact undetected.

She and I actually had a negative encounter one day during my first few weeks there. We were both in the kitchen at work and she passed me in a harsh manner and didn't speak. It kind of shocked me as a contrast to her typical kind and friendly demeanor, even though I shouldn't have been surprised because of my previous transgressions against her. However, later that day she came to my desk and apologized to me for how she behaved in the kitchen. She said, even given the circumstances, she should not have acted that way towards me. Although I was the one who was doing her wrong, here I was accepting her apology. After she left my desk, I picked up the phone and called the Pastor and told him what transpired. He told me that was my opportunity to apologize to her, but I missed it. Then, I called her husband and told him what had happened. He told me to lay low for a little bit.

One day, my husband and I were going on a double date with him and his wife to a baseball game. He and my husband were actually friends, close buddies. Consequently, it hurt my husband when he found out that I had previously sent him inappropriate pictures. But, since I took the fall for it, I lied, and said I was the one trying to come on to him—he got off the hook and my husband never knew that we had other interactions. After that situation blew over, my husband tried to rekindle their friendship.

The day of the game, he told me to get off work early and come to their house before his wife got off. I went to their house early. After learning that his kids weren't home, I hugged him, then we kissed, and one thing led to another. He had already slipped his hands under the dress I was wearing and pulled off my underwear while fondling me. He then pulled me to the floor right there in their living room, and tried to lay me down, but I stopped him and got on top of him instead. It was brief because I stopped it as soon as we started. Even though I didn't care about much, it still felt wrong to be doing that in their house and right before we were going out together with our spouses.

Then I left the house, returned after his wife got home from work, and changed my clothes while we waited for my husband's arrival so we could all go to the game. Imagine the guilt that plagued me during the date at the baseball game. And he and I sat next to each other with our spouses on the outside ends of us. Since I had been aroused earlier, I kept trying to be close to him, sneaking in touches by rubbing my leg against his, and leaning over onto him in laughter during funny moments. My husband actually noticed something was going on but he didn't say anything until much later.

Then he went through a rough time in his marriage and during that time, he admitted to his wife that he'd cheated on her, for years with other women. I had already known this about him because he'd told me. That caused them to go through counseling to repair their marriage. He told me she admitted she wasn't fulfilling her wifely duties and would do better. Then, he made the decision to be baptized to be cleansed from his sins. After that, he told me that he wanted to move on from me and wanted to cut all communications between us. I understood and obliged. We would only see one another at church, but didn't really engage in conversation; we only offered brief greetings. But, I silently wondered if it would last. It didn't.

That moment of marital restoration for them and his time away from me was short-lived. A few months later, one day we happened to be at the church together on a Tuesday. I was there for dance rehearsal and he was there with his wife while she was at Praise & Worship rehearsal. He started to flirt with me, which struck me as odd.

Then at one point I had to run out to my car, I went out through the back lobby entrance. With him being security, he watched me. The lights weren't on in the lobby, so it was dark. When I came back in, he got up close to me, rubbing on my booty. He too was a booty man. I asked what was up with him and his wife and he stated that his wife had reverted back to her old ways, and the sex was limited again. This reminded me of the statement often made to girlfriends and wives, "What you won't do, another woman will." I know that to be true on both ends of the spectrum, as a wife and as a mistress. He was an extremely sexual, strong-natured man, and had to have it. From this brief interaction, we started back talking again, more frequently.

He picked his wife up from work and there would be times when I would go out to see him before she got out of the building to leave. We'd be talking or texting and he'd tell me that he was arriving and I'd go out for a quick break just to see him. Or he would tell her he would be late, but actually come at the right time and he would pick me up and we'd go for a brief chat and moment to see one another.

It was Halloween night one year and we were at church for the Hallelujah Night, which we held as an alternative to Halloween for the kids. I was there as a volunteer, he was there as security, and his wife was there with their kid and grandkids. He and I were texting one another through the night even though we were in the same building. During the course of our texting, we made plans to meet at the end of the night. As the night wound down, he sent his family home. After his family left, we left. We met at a secluded spot and we had sex that night in his truck. After that night, we had a full-fledged sexual relationship that continued for many months, almost up until a year later.

There were times I would leave work on my lunch break and go to his job to have sex with him and come back to work and have to see his wife. Of course, I felt guilty. His wife was a really sweet, endearing, and accepting woman. I had no hard feelings against her. It's just that I was strongly attracted to her husband, especially sexually. I would always try to stay away from her, hoping that she couldn't smell her husband's scent on me. Treacherous, I know, but I was strongly being controlled by the lust of my flesh and this man was very sexually fulfilling, literally. Sometimes we had lunch together when we didn't have sex. We were able to see one another and it not be about sex.

Since I started seeing those two members again, my strong affinity for the Pastor had waned, mainly because he didn't give me what I wanted, and I was getting it elsewhere. He still had a part of my heart though. I still interacted with him, but it, too, was a masquerade to make it seem like I was still into him so that my actions with the others wouldn't be discovered.

My husband worked excessively, so I had a lot of free time on my hands. I used to call myself a single wife because of the amount of time I spent by myself. This guy and I both loved to workout, he more so than I, and he was extremely physically fit. Mostly because of his security business, he stayed in great shape. I had a gym membership, but he had a make-shift gym at one of the empty commercial spaces at the property he worked at. He loved that I liked to workout, something that his wife didn't like to do, and she was a much larger woman than I was. Everyday after work, I went to the gym. In effort to see him more, I asked him if he would be my personal trainer, which he excitedly agreed to. Therefore, I would tell my husband that I was going to the gym after work but I was actually going to his gym on the days he was available. He and I enjoyed working out together. He trained me. He was an extreme hard trainer with no mercy at all, and I couldn't be a wimp while working out with him. We would do workouts together, and also meet up to go running at the bayou near his house which was close to our job.

He built and sculpted my body into the body he wished his wife had. It was torture for me, but I let him do it, anything for me to be able to be with him. He was a really hard and strict trainer but I got the results. My husband hated him at this point because sometime prior, he found out about our interactions through my iPad and he couldn't believe that his friend had the nerve to mess with this wife. Because of this, his messing around with me in this manner was like "sticking it" to my husband. He was being spiteful towards my husband intentionally. Even though I knew this, I let it continue. I know that was wrong of me. One day, he joked that my husband should thank him for my body that he built. I had gotten really toned and sexy, and I have the pictures to prove it. *Wink.

But of course our sessions were more than workouts. We had sex there too, all the time. Before working out, or just meet up to have sex and no workout. One time, we had sex the night before he was going away on an anniversary trip with his wife. There was a time his wife had gone out of town for a family function, and we met up there to have sex. One time, we had sex the day before I was going away on a trip with my husband. We were actually going away to my college graduation to be exact. We met up that evening, but I told him I didn't want to have sex that night. I had a fear of flying and I felt like I needed to be sin-free before getting up in the air in an airplane. He laughed at me and told me all I had to do was repent. He refused to let me go away on my trip without him getting some. Of course that meant I couldn't have sex with husband on that trip and I didn't. Thankfully, our daughter shared a room with us and therefore I didn't have to make an excuse why I couldn't. We even had sex when I was on my menstrual cycles. He said he liked it more that way because it made me wetter. I didn't like it, but it was extremely difficult to tell him no.

One day we met up and he expressed that it would probably be our last time having sex because he and his wife were now a part of the Marriage Ministry team. Him telling me this was kind of a gut punch for a couple of reasons. One, why wasn't my husband and I asked to be a part of the marriage ministry team? As a matter of fact, previously I was over the Marriage ministry. Two, how could they pick a couple with the husband committing adultery. How would they even know you may ask? It's call spiritual discernment. As a matter of fact, another low blow was another couple chosen to be a part of the marriage ministry team was my godson's parents.. Crazy huh? Here you have two husbands committing adultery with the same woman, and now they are both a part of the church's marriage team. It didn't matter that by this time, I was more into the security guy than my godson's father but all our interactions hadn't ended. More importantly, the fact remains that the newly appointed marriage team members were in no spiritual or moral position to take on those roles and that bothered me.

I knew this man was using me for his own sexual fulfillment, but I was enjoying it because I was being sexually fulfilled as well. My sex life with my husband was dry and unfulfilling, even before adding these guys to the equation. Don't get me wrong, there was more between us than sex. Remember, we spent several years talking as friends. Our camaraderie was great. We had tremendously good, deep conversations, especially when talking about our ambitions, dreams, and goals. Which included him furthering his education for a new career, whereas I fully supported him in this endeavor. After he graduated, I rewarded him for his accomplishment. Don't get me wrong, I too supported my husband in everything he did career-wise. As a visionary, I absolutely show support to anyone who has vision or endeavors for growth & advancement.

At one point, we even talked about getting an apartment together as our getaway spot. We even talked about how we probably couldn't make it as a married couple. He was too demanding and domineering. I was really stubborn and strong-willed. His wife was passive and a submissive woman. I wasn't quite there yet. We knew we were better as friends and sex partners. By the way, he didn't stop having sex with me after joining the marriage ministry. He said he couldn't stay away. Go figure.

I even recall a time my daughter gave me information pertaining to this man's daughter. I immediately called the Pastor and disclosed the information to him because she was singing on the praise and worship team. Of course they had a talk with her and she was removed from the team. When I look back on it, how could I tell on her when, at that time, I was having an affair with both her father and another man at the church, and the latter was also the godfather of her children. This was typical, hypocritical behavior, throwing stones at others and while committing sexual sin myself. My reason for mentioning this behavior isn't just about me; sadly, it happens in churches all the time.

Our relationship ended abruptly after I had quickly gotten into a very bad place in my marriage and it had become further broken, almost irreparable, mainly due to my indiscretions because I no longer cared about my marriage, my husband, or even my relationship with God. I wanted to leave my husband, but he didn't want me to go.

I told my husband that I was leaving him and was going to get my own apartment. This was also an attempt to leave the church and God. He didn't want to let that happen because he knew that I was up to no good, although he had no proof, and this time, I refused to admit it. Still, he didn't want me to leave. My husband told the Pastor about his alleged concerns of my indiscretions and the Pastor and his wife had an extremely harsh talk with me. I was really defiant and didn't want to hear anything they had to say. Accordingly, my husband and I made a mutual agreement and instead, I took a leave of absence from my marriage and went to Houston, TX for a personal "Revival" with

God.

God was not going to let me stay in the sin that I thrust myself in and He actually exposed me or you could say, He rescued me from my rebellion according to Psalm 39:8 (NLT), *"Rescue me from my rebellion. Do not let fools mock me."* How did God expose me? One day, I was working from home. During my lunch break hour, I went to visit a male neighbor down the street who I'd become friends with. As I was walking up to the house, I clearly heard Holy Spirit say, "Don't go in that house." I didn't heed the warning. Because of my disobedience, a simple visit turned into a 4-hour, hostage like situation because I got stuck in that house as my husband ended up coming home during a work break. When I wasn't at the house, my daughter told him she didn't know where I was and that she thought I went walking as I normally did.

When my husband couldn't find me out walking, he came and knocked on the neighbor's door looking for me as he suspected I was there. The neighbor lied and told him I wasn't there. I wanted to try to get out, but the neighbor wouldn't let me. No, it wasn't a sex visit and we didn't have sex. Of course, my husband didn't believe that was the case. All he figured was his wife was in that house. I stayed trapped in there until the neighbor snuck me into the back of his vehicle, drove me far away from our neighborhood, dropped me off and I had to walk all the way home.

After that moment, its like God let everything concerning me to be bared before my husband and everyone. I had been using a flip phone to interact with member #2 and the neighbor, and when my husband found it, he flipped. He confronted them both and they both denied our interactions being anything more than platonic. I endured much hardship because of my actions but more importantly my action of not heeding to the voice and warning of God.

One weekend, my daughter couldn't endure the intensity of the constant fighting in our home and she asked a church member if she could stay with them. After I dropped her off, too afraid to stay home alone with my husband, I snuck and stayed at the neighbors house. I was afraid to be alone with my husband after a terrifying incident that occurred following my exposure. One night I was in the shower, as I was bathing, I saw a red dot on the ceramic tile of the shower wall. I turned to see my husband pointing a gun directly at me. Scared, I asked what was he doing? He said to me, "How does it make you feel having this gun pointed at you?" And asked if I hurt like he hurt me. I told him, "No." I told him if he was to pull that trigger and shoot me, I couldn't heal from the hurt being dead, but he could eventually heal from the hurt I caused him. Eventually, my husband awakened from his temporary moment of insanity and went and called my mother told her what he'd done. Not only did he put fear in me, but he put fear in my mother of what he could do to me.

While staying at the neighbors house, my husband actually found my car where I had parked it in a parking lot away from the house and I wasn't home, he had my car towed to the house and hid it in the garage, and locked me out. I told him that I stayed at a motel in the area and hid my car so that he wouldn't find me. Of course I begged him to let me come back home, he did but only for the night.

Convinced that I was cheating on him, he sent me to stay with his mother until he could figure out, "What to do with me." Even during that brief period, going through this with my husband, I still talked to member #2 while at my mother-in-law's house. While I was there one night, his wife was at praise & worship rehearsal, so he tried to get me to come to his house so that we could be together. I declined because it was going to be too risky with the kids in the house, but he insisted I come anyway. Still having to get my workout in, I walked to an area park to workout and we were going to meet afterwards. However, it didn't happen, he ended up falling asleep and missed my phone calls. That was probably my last time talking to him before

I went away.

God had a purpose and calling for my life and was going to make sure that I reached it and that I did not destroy myself. This exposure caused me to become immensely broken and bitter with God, but I still made the decision to yield to God's will for my life. I had been living in full sin and rebellion against God and my husband, all the while masquerading around in the church and amongst family and friends as if I was the perfect Christian woman. Quite the opposite, I was a woman who had an affair with the Pastor, committed adultery with two of the members, and engaging with a non-Christian man. I was out there bad.

CHAPTER 11

Deliverance

My true deliverance came after I left my home, husband, daughter, job, and the church and went away for six-weeks. At that time, God had exposed me in my sin and I became broken. In that place of brokenness, according to Psalm 34:18 (NLT), *"The Lord is close to the brokenhearted; he rescues those whose spirits are crushed,"* I experienced the true love, grace, mercy, and forgiveness of God. God had gotten me exactly where He wanted me. It was in that place that I received true deliverance from the perverse spirits, and from the spirit of rejection, and I became whole and restored.

I spent an entire 6-weeks in partial seclusion while staying with one of my sisters. She was the only person who had complete access to me and God used her to speak life into me as I was going through my brokenness. Morning to night, I listened to the word of God. I mainly listened to messages on grace, forgiveness, and restoration by Pastor Creflo Dollar. I filled myself with these teachings. I listened to praise & worship music when I was not listening to teachings. I spent a lot of time in prayer with periods of fasting. My job allowed me to work remotely during this period, and that allowed me to be in a safe, quiet space.

My only activities during this time took place at church. Of course, this was nothing like my past behavior in the church. God had me on a strict regimen. When I packed for my getaway, God gave me specific instructions not to take any items of vanity. I couldn't pack my Christian Louboutin shoes, nor my Louis Vuitton or Gucci handbags. I took only a few Michael Kors items. For Sunday worship and Wednesday bible study, I attended services at the mega-church I was a member of before I had gotten married and left Houston. The Pastor and First Lady there embraced me lovingly through this period and also yielded counsel to me for my healing and restoration. The word that was being taught over the pulpit were also messages I needed to hear to renew me and strengthen me in faith again.

I went to church on Wednesday, Friday, Saturday, and Sunday each week. I also only went to the gym with my sister because I was still following my workout regimen. I also did this to help my sister live an active lifestyle in addition to cooking healthy meals for us. I had no other activities except for the one time I did community service to feed the homeless on the streets of Houston. This was also a life-changing, exhilarating experience. I was allowed one trip to the mall, on Labor Day, but it was to shop for something very specific. I had limited visitations from family and friends; I saw two friends once and another sister once. In my last week, I drove out of town to visit my oldest sister and brother. I rarely even saw my mom during this period. It was all about revival with God.

I went through deliverance and restoration until God had done a complete work in me. I then had to transform my thinking of how I felt about myself and be free from the low self-esteem and feelings of insignificance I had about myself. During this process of deliverance, God transformed my thinking of how I saw myself with two specific scriptures. Genesis 1:26 (NIV), *"Then God said, Let us make mankind in our image, in our likeness..."* When I read that scripture with the revelation of what God was showing me, my thinking changed immediately. I began to think, "If I'm made in the image and likeness of God, there is no way I could have low self-esteem and there was no way that I could consider myself to be insignificant. There was nothing insignificant about God and what He's created, especially me!" Then I read Psalms 139:14, *"I praise you because I am fearfully and wonderfully made; your works are wonderful, I know that full well."* In reading this scripture, the revelation I received about myself is that God made me, my spirit man, exactly who I am. The way I looked may be a byproduct of features from my mother and father but my looks do not define who I am.

From that moment forward, I looked at myself differently and I began to love myself differently because in that same moment, I realized God's love for me wasn't based on how I looked. He loved me as His daughter based on my spirit and the condition of my heart, and how I lived for Him. I had been cleansed by the blood of Jesus. After this transformation in my mind about how I thought about myself, I no longer needed makeup. Now, when I wear makeup, it's because of my love for it and creativity when using it on myself or others when working as a makeup artist. I also changed the way I dressed. I stopped dressing for sex appeal and attention, but I dressed as a woman more confident in herself and as a representative of Christ. I didn't change my style of dress because I am definitely one who has style, but I just changed my focus and intention of why I wear the outfits I choose.

I knew the work of God was completed in me when my sister asked me to go to a Rosh Hosanna weekend service with her that year. At that service something happened to me and through me that changed the trajectory of my life. The first thing that happened was I ministered a prophetic dance, which I'd never done before. The next thing that happened was I was mantled by the guest Apostle at the service and she prophesied over my life and awakened the prophetic gift in me. I had never been prophesied to before. I'd seen prophecy take place and I had a strong draw to Prophets, not knowing it was because of the gift and call within me.

The last thing was that I released everything and everybody from the previous period of my life, including the burden of remorse and guilt I carried for what I'd done towards God, my husband, my godson's mother, the praise & worship leader, and even the Pastor's wife. I walked out of that weekend of service in complete liberty. I was free, even from the soul-ties from not only the Pastor, but also with the other two men and anyone else I was tied to from my past. During one of the services, I was even instructed by God to give away the pair of Michael Kors shoes I had worn to service, which I had gotten just before I went to Houston.

The last thing that happened was my husband flew into town and we renewed our vows at a mass Wedding and Vow renewal service my church in Houston had. It was a unique and beautiful service. I just knew this was a new start, new beginning for us, but it didn't exactly happen as I envisioned. As a matter of fact, my husband and I had a fight in the airport the next day on our way home. At that point, I should have stayed in Houston, renewed vows or not, but instead I got on the plane with him and returned home.

When I returned home, I was different. My mindset was different. My worship was different. My love walk was different. My conversation was different. My discernment was different; it was more keen. A lot of the church members noticed this difference in me. Several broken relationships with female members had been restored after my return and new relationships were formed. Even my relationship with the praise & worship leader was restored.

At first, when I left for Houston, the Pastor didn't hear from me. He found out from my husband where I was.

My husband told me that the Pastor was really mad at me because I didn't tell him that I was leaving. The reason I didn't tell him was because I wanted to make the decision on my own. For many years prior to my revival, I had allowed the Pastor, along with his wife sometimes to counsel me and to influence a lot of decisions I made, especially the decisions to stay with my husband when I felt that I should have left; especially following his infidelity. The Pastor influenced my decision to accept the permanent position when offered, of the temporary job that I really hated, and to make many other decisions that affected my household. During my last week of being away, Holy Spirit impressed upon me to give him a call. He answered, we talked, and I could tell he was hurt. He was very angry and upset with me and he let it be known. He didn't talk to me nicely at all. We ended the call after only a few minutes of talking. But, I was led to call back and apologize for how it made him feel by me not letting him know that I was leaving. After the apology, our conversation changed and we began to talk for a while, like we were friends again. However, my conversation was different.

Following my restoration, I grew in my relationship with God and myself. I no longer looked to man during troubled times, not even my husband. God was my sole confidant. I learned to have a healthy, whole relationship with myself where I loved me and became content with who I had become, and it did not matter if others wanted a relationship with me. I embraced the fact that I was an introvert, and an anti-social one at that. I was really different.

When I returned home, the Pastor and I would still talk on the phone a lot but this time, I was talking more about the word, God's grace, and restoration. Then, it happened. I guess it was a test. He slipped in his subtle sexual innuendo, and I let it pass. In later conversations, he did it again and I still did not take the bait. His response, "You really have changed." "Yes I have, and I'm so excited about it," was my response. That's when he began to change. He started to pull back from me. Apparently, my deliverance was intimidating to him. Our telephone calls now became infrequent. My access to him at church was either limited or non-existent. But then the spirit of the Lord opened my eyes, the spirit of discernment rested upon me, and I saw it all so clearly.

I saw the spirit of perversion and lust so heavy in that church and it began to suffocate me. Whenever I would get the opportunity to talk to the Pastor, I would tell him that I needed to leave the church, to which he would always respond, "No," regardless of the reason I gave to leave. On top of that, I was growing differently in my renewed relationship with God like never before. I felt like I was a new babe in Christ. I had learned about the Prophetic call on my life and I started growing and developing in that area. The Apostle who prophesied over me in the Rosh Hosanna service told me something very specific. She said in January, a change was going to take place in my life.

When January came, that is when it was first spoken to me about the prophetic gift I possessed and that word kept coming to me from other leaders and prophets. I also started learning about deliverance ministry, knowing that God was drawing me there as well. Then, the Pastor and I started bumping heads again, but this time it was because our views on the prophetic and deliverance were different, but more so because of my own personal experience with deliverance. I wanted to leave the church so badly, but he wouldn't "release me," so-to-speak. He insisted that I needed to stay and be "taught from the pulpit," he told me one time. "Proper" church protocol dictates that when you plan to leave the church, the Pastor should be in agreement with it and "release" you with his or her blessing. This generally happens when a Pastor is secure and wants the best for the people to ensure that they are following God and His purpose for their lives, whether it is at that Pastor's church or not. Unfortunately, this was just not going to happen for me.

CHAPTER 12

Replaced

*H*ow long will I continue to protect them? That was a question that kept coming up in my spirit. It was obvious who the woman I saw as the Pastor's replacement for me because the two of them had begun to grow very close, just as he and I had, especially due to her "leadership position." Just as my position did, there were areas of her position which too required approvals by him before anything could be implemented. I admit that seeing him with her week after week, knowing that she replaced me did make me jealous. I kind of missed our relationship and I let it be known to him, but he teased me about being jealous of he and the other woman's relationship. When I would see him with her or another other woman who was in the picture in ways that I saw him with me, I would try to intercept, or "cock block" as it used to be said. I was trying to prevent him from being with them the way he previously was with me. But I didn't do this because of jealousy. I was trying to prevent him from being exposed. Then one day, Holy Spirit checked me. He told me that I was not his wife and I could not protect him. I was then hands off and started to back off completely.

I remember when I saw him with the woman I suspected to be my replacement one day after service. She and he were in the sound room of the church, just like I recall our time in the sound room. I happened to be passing by the window to the room and the Holy Spirit had me to hone in; it was like the curtain was opened for me to see. The Pastor was sitting in the chair, the same way he was sitting that day, years prior, the chair I had straddled him in, in the exact same spot. She was standing very close to him and they were conversing. But what I noticed most was the body language between the two of them. He was looking at her the same way he used to look at me and she was giving him the same type of attention I used to give him. That moment confirmed that I had truly been replaced, and by her. As a result, I didn't like her and I made it known to him. I actually didn't like her prior to that moment, more so because she was given a position that required her to work closely with him before I went away for my deliverance.

He reveled in the fact that I was jealous of seeing him with another "other woman," and he marveled at it. If they ever were together and I was passing by them or in their vicinity, he would jokingly pull her in close, snidely say, "Hi" to me, and say, "Here's such and such" saying her name while having a huge smile spread across his face. And a scowl would spread across my face. I must admit, although delivered, he apparently still had a small inkling of my heart. I guess my going back to that church showed that maybe I wasn't completely free of him.

He did the joking behavior not only with her, but with another woman he often spent time with around the church, whom I didn't like either. My disdain for her, too, was the result of a conversation I overheard them having before my deliverance. The two of them were sitting in the last row at the back of the sanctuary conversing. I was standing behind him, in my usual, being close to him manner. His wife wasn't around. While they were talking, all of sudden

I heard him say, "Why couldn't I have met you 33 years ago." Her response was a chuckle. I was shocked at hearing him say that. First, it said to me that the conversation was very personal, but secondly, I interpreted him saying that as to say, why he couldn't have met her prior to marrying his wife. Or, if he would have met her, he wouldn't have married his wife. From that moment forward, I watched their relationship flourish strongly. When I questioned the Pastor on his relationship with her, "I'm working with her on something," was his response. "Why can't your wife work with her?" was my jealous reply. I even expressed my observation to the Pastor's son and nephew of which they both assured me there was nothing to be concerned about due to a specific characteristic. However, I witnessed their relationship grow closer.

When that perverse spirit is gone, it no longer attracts those who still have it. I noticed that the men in the church who I used to play and joke around with no longer engaged me in such activity. And I even noticed who became my replacement with them. She was a pretty single woman, very friendly, but most of all, had a big butt and it got all the men's attention, including the Pastor. I even witnessed him make comments about her butt. One day, I rebuked him as I felt led by the Holy Spirit to do, for how he interacted and talked inappropriately with these women. He told me that I couldn't rebuke him, but I did with authority. After that conversation we had, I later noticed he backed off from how he interacted with those women, albeit short-lived.

I observed how this other lady responded and acted with the guys around the church, exactly the same way I had. I recall the Holy Spirit did tell me to talk to her about it, but I didn't, thinking she would deny anything was even there. But having been influenced by that same spirit and engaging with the guys in the same manner she had, I recognized it. I even recognized that the praise & worship leader's husband's interactions with this lady had apparently replaced mine. Every time I saw certain exchanges between the two, I would try to intervene. Even a couple of times I tried to divert his attention back to me. I don't know if it was jealousy or protection, but either way, he didn't need to be engaging with her. Once again, Holy Spirit checked me. He told me that I was not his wife and I could not protect him. And again, I backed off.

This lady even seemed to be replacing me with my husband while I was still there. I found inappropriate text messages between the two of them on his cell phone, and saw they communicated often. He'd even taken inappropriate pictures with her at his birthday party I found on his cell phone; one with his hand around her waist and his head nestled into the crook of her neck. If you would have seen the pictures he and I took that night, you could have fit another person in the middle of us, that's how distant he was from me. I also found out he had taken her along to a baseball game that was supposed to have been with her older son who my husband was supposed to be mentoring because of her son's behavioral issues. This struck me hard, because she and I were supposedly BFF's and I didn't understand how you were going to a baseball game with my husband and didn't say anything to me. Even after the fact, she never mentioned going. But apparently, my husband's mentoring filtered over into a liking of the mother. My finding out about their behavior caused me to confront my husband and ended in a violent physical altercation between us.

I remember this particular day, the Pastor and I were on a phone call. In that conversation I talked about my calling as a Prophetess. He asked me, "Did God give you a scripture to confirm this call?" I replied, "Yes." He was insisting that I show him the scripture, but another call had come in, so he had to end our call and told me he would call me back expecting the scripture. When I hung up the phone, I clearly heard Holy Spirit tell me strongly "You will not." Then He told me to cut **all** interactions with him. At first I tried to ignore it but Holy Spirit quickly reminded me that my purpose and my calling was far greater than any illegal, inappropriate, unrighteous relationship with this man.

My spiritual eyes were opening more and more. All respect for the Pastor had been lost because I knew and saw who he really was: a predator to the weak and broken. These other two women were broken. I discerned that he preyed on broken women and that caused me to recall other women in the church he'd had close relationships with. When he saw I was no longer broken and no longer needed his counsel or consoling for brokenness, he no longer wanted to interact with me on a personal basis. I could no longer listen to anything he had to say. I couldn't focus in service or listen to his teachings. A friend of mine had met him once, briefly, and she immediately said, "He has no anointing, no oil at all, and you need to get away from him." I realized, she was right. The **only** reason I kept going to that church was because I was forced to. To keep some form of peace in my home with my husband who wouldn't let me leave the church either, I submitted because he threatened we'd have to divorce me I went to another church. He was all about appearance.

I further lost respect for the Pastor when a situation came up with our financial giving statement for my husband and me one particular year. When we received the statement, it was off by thousands of dollars. I told my husband and he brought it to the attention of the Pastor's wife. Since the Pastor and I still talked sporadically, I called him to let him know what was going on. I blew a gasket when he had the nerve to say that if our tithes and offerings weren't recorded, we didn't give. I was livid. Why would I make a fuss about something if I didn't do it? But I was telling the truth, and that's why Holy Spirit had my back.

That year, I had started giving in cash because it took too long for checks written to the church to clear my bank. However, Holy Spirit told me to record my giving on the calendar on my iPad which I did for any Sunday or Wednesday tithes and offerings. I was able to go back through the year and found that our Sunday tithes, which was large dollar amounts given in cash, were missing from being recorded from March to August. The Sunday giving wasn't recorded again until September. Only the $10 or $20 Wednesday offerings were on the statement. Apparently, an investigation found something going on because my husband was told to give the Church Administrator the dates and amounts missing and we were given a revised statement with no further explanation. During a phone conversation we were having, the Pastor actually mentioned to me that the same thing happened to another member and their giving statement, but told me not to say anything to anyone.

CHAPTER 13

Repent & Release

I was still going to church at the demand of my husband, but I was so turned off by the Pastor and his teaching. I had been telling my husband that I needed to leave that church and get into one that was an apostolic/prophetic ministry, one that could help cultivate me in my prophetic gift. But he refused. I even asked if I could go to a School of the Prophets to learn and grow in my gift, and he refused that too. I don't think he believed in my calling. As a matter of fact, my husband didn't even believe that I was transformed. He treated me badly, and our relationship grew worse instead of better during the two years following my return. I worked hard at becoming a better woman, and especially a better wife. I sought counsel and help to be better and implemented the things I was told and wisdom I received, but it was not received or reciprocated. I can admit that I was a piece of work, but when I made the decision to change; change I did. I even told my husband one day, "God gave you the wife you'd been asking for on a silver platter and served her to you and you're throwing me back into God's face like you don't want me." But others in the church saw the new, transformed me and they let me know and told me how happy they were for me. Even my daughter marveled at the transformed me. My husband did admit that he noticed the changes I was making; however, he didn't treat me better as a result.

As a matter of fact, the Praise & Worship Leader— the woman whose husband and I had an affair—and I actually began to talk and connect more after my return. I had no guilt and condemnation talking to her because I was delivered and free. One day, she told me that God told her to tell me that I had truly been transformed and even if others didn't believe it and recognize, transformation had happened in me. I was grateful for that. God even gave me the opportunity to repent to her for my inappropriate interactions with her husband, although I did not confess about us having full infidelity. However, from that point, she and I grew in a relationship that really showed what forgiveness and the grace of God looked like. I even wrote a book, using her and her testimony as the muse and foundation for the book, *One Hot Summer.*

One day, I asked my husband if I could go to another church and he flat out said that if I went to a different church, we'd have to get a divorce. Well, I didn't want to get a divorce, as we'd just renewed our vows almost two years prior. For that reason, I "submitted" to my husband and went to church with him every Wednesday for Bible Study and every Sunday for service. But I refused to go to any extra activities.

About one month prior to my departure from the ministry, finally, during his teaching from the pulpit, the Pastor looked me dead in my eyes and said, "I will not release you!" Hearing that hurt like a knife had just been thrust through my heart. I put my head down as tears welled up in my eyes. He continued, "I love you too much to let you leave." Then he adds, "And that man loves you more than you'll ever know," referring to my husband sitting next to me. That was really hard to believe he was saying that, knowing for years he'd betrayed my husband, his friend-ship, and many acts of kindness, love and appreciation to-wards him as the Pastor and his family by having an affair with his wife…for years!

Even during this service, prior to telling me that he wouldn't release me, the Pastor even publicly revealed the "brokenness" the other two women dealt with because of their past, which confirmed my discernment that he preyed on the broken. After service that day, I was ready to get up out of there. I made a beeline to the door but got caught in fellowship with members while saying bye. As I made it to the door, I just so happened to be approaching at the same time as the Pastor was coming in that direction.

He said sarcastically, "You know I love you girl," through a big smile on his face.

I said, "Yeah, but I still have to leave. You don't believe in what God has called me to do, and I can't stay here."

He asked what was that? I responded, "The prophetic and deliverance."

One time in a conversation, the Pastor had told me that Prophets were not necessary in the church in this day be-cause we know have Holy Spirit and that I needed to show him scripture to prove that Prophets were a necessity in the church. Of course I told him Ephesians 4:11, but more importantly, 1 Corinthians 12:28. And I reiterated how that scripture said, *"And God has placed in the church first of all apostles, second prophets, third teachers…"* He, himself was a Pastor/Teacher and so I told him that scripture proves that Prophets took precedence over him in the church. This proved how unlearned he was in this area regarding the prophetic and prophets and why I really needed to leave. His comment proved that he had nothing to teach me.

Then he said, "Deliverance is not what you think it is, just sit here and I will teach you from the pulpit." I knew what deliverance was, I had witnessed it, experienced it, and was now studying it.

Oh no, I thought as I gave him a very disagreeing look.

"Don't you trust that I can hear God for you?" he replied to my unspoken words.

"No!" I said flat out.

He was quite shocked at my response. He positioned himself directly in front of me, close to my face looked me square in the eyes and asked "Why Not?" I believe he knew what was coming, but probably was looking to see if I was bold enough to say it and I did.

"Because you violated me," I responded.

He went into even more shock when I said that. Then he asked "How? Are you saying I touched you?"

"Yes," I said.

He said, "No I didn't. How? When?"

"All the years of the things we did when I worked with you at the church and thereafter," I said.

He went into an immediate tizzy and defense and denial mode. He started to get loud. I remained quiet and calm and kept telling him to lower his voice because people didn't need to hear what we were talking about, including his armor bearer who was in close proximity to us.

He proceeds to say, "I can call my wife over here and you can say this in front of her."

"She doesn't need to come over here, this is between me and you," I responded.

I was not angry or hostile in any way, I just responded truthfully. At that point, he now needed to be responsible for his actions, repent, and release me. But, it never happened. He stormed off in anger, but before he did, he asked,

"Did you have any other interactions with other men in this church?"

"Yes, you know that!" I said.

"Who?" he asked, and then quickly changed and said, "I don't want to know," and stomped off angrily.

On the drive home from church, I wanted to tell my husband everything that transpired, but for some reason Holy Spirit would not allow me to. I had to remain silent. The next week, I was made to go back to church. I refused to go to bible study though. On Sunday's, my husband and I sat in the same seats every week. That next Sunday, we were moved a row back from our usual seats and there was a security guard now stationed directly behind the Pastor right in front of us. I didn't catch on until the following Sunday that something strange was going on. I told my husband, what I observed. Telling him, "Look, he's increased his security." My husband brushed it off. He only knew of what happened the previous Sunday, when the Pastor said he would not release me, and knew that I'd be mad about not being able to leave the church, but not knowing the events that occurred after service were cause of the tension between the Pastor and me. Then I began to notice that security followed my every move. I wasn't even thinking about the Pastor or that church. I was the last person they needed security for.

Although I was made to come, I still participated in worship because worship to God was where I got my peace and strength. I never listened to anything the Pastor said as he was teaching though. I was doing my own personal bible study and writing messages for my Facebook Live broadcasts. Although every now and again I would look up, nod my head to make it look like I was paying attention to keep peace between my husband and me. I had to do this because he said I was being rebellious when it was really because he didn't know all that was going on.

Coming up to Easter Sunday, the Pastor started teaching a message about Judas' betrayal and how people will betray you. He said in the first installment of this teaching series, "The person sitting on the side of you is likely to betray you." I discerned really quickly that he was talking about me. I leaned over to my husband and said, "He's talking about me." My husband was perturbed at me saying that. He sensed there were some issues between me and the Pastor, but because I couldn't talk about it, he turned against me and sided with the Pastor. According to him, the Pastor was right and I was out of order.

Sunday after Sunday, I was made to go to that church and sit and listen to that Pastor talk about me indirectly from the pulpit in his messages. I had to endure it all, and "suffer in silence." One day on the car ride home, I asked my husband, "If someone who you really esteemed, honored, and called a friend was messing around with your wife, would you feel that person betrayed you?" He didn't answer the question with a yes or no response but asked questions about what I was trying to say. Then I asked, "If your wife decided to tell you she messed around with that person, would she be betraying that person?" Once again, he wanted me to give him details, but I just wanted to get his perspective on who was really being betrayed. As well, I was trying to tell him about me and the Pastor's past escapades and how he betrayed him, but once again Holy Spirit prompted me to be silent.

One Sunday, my husband went out of town, and I was so excited! That meant I was going to get the opportunity to go and visit the church I'd been wanting to attend. However, Holy Spirit told me "No," and said that I'm to go to my own church. He even showed me in a vision where I'd be seated. I was so discouraged, but I had to be obedient to Holy Spirit. I went to church. The ushers saw that I was alone and seated me on a different row, but it was exactly where Holy Spirit showed me in the vision. I was seated on the second row behind the Pastor, about 2 seats down from him. I chuckled at this and was in awe that I saw it in a vision.

In his sermon, the Pastor said something that I disagreed with and I leaned over to my neighbor and made a quick comment. I used her as stand in for my husband because that's what I always did with him. With him, I always leaned over to comment on something that was said that I didn't agree with or ask a question about it. The Pastor actually saw the exchange happen and had the nerve to call us out in the midst of his sermon, but we didn't say anything. Then…he said, "If you have an issue with something

I said, you can come see me." I had absolutely no problem with that. After service ended, I marched myself right up to him with my issue. Of course his increased security plus his wife were right there "to protect him," but I didn't care. I took him up on his offer. He had said this quite a few times in his messages before, but I think he did that as a scare tactic to people.

In that moment, we got into a disagreement about what I told him my issue was. Towards the end of his sermon, the Pastor asked if the Periscope and Facebook Live had been turned off. His response made me think the broadcasters said yes, because he said that they should have left it on because "those devils" watching on there needed to hear what he was saying. He literally had just said in his message, that we, the members, can't talk negatively about people. And, he turns around and does it himself, calling people devils. In my personal opinion, I think he was referring to people who no longer attended the ministry but watched the broadcast. However, he was wrong for saying that and I let him know. I flatly stated that he said we have to watch what we're saying about people and then turned around and did the very thing himself by calling people devils. "You don't know them, but you can't be saying that," is what I told him. Of course he disagreed. He kept saying, "They are devils," and I kept saying, "But you can't call them that." He was getting very angry. Thus, his protector— his wife, pushed him away in the opposite direction from me and I left.

Little did I know that would be my last Sunday there, but God knew. I think that is why He made me go. I had only been paying my tithes there, but I refused to give any offerings or sow any seeds there. Once again, BUT GOD! He already had me planting seeds in other places, ministries, and people of integrity, setting me up for a pure harvest.

The next Sunday was Mother's Day. I didn't intend to miss church, but it happened. I had arrived back in town from Washington, DC very late in the evening and I was hosting a celebration barbecue at my house that Sunday for my niece who'd graduated from Howard University the previous day. Additionally, I had also started getting my hair braided after the graduation festivities and it still wasn't finished when it was time for church, so I didn't go. This infuriated my husband. Little did I know that day would also be my last day with my husband as well. Once again, BUT GOD!

He came home very late after church, although he knew he had to prepare the meat and other dishes for our dinner party. It was a little tense between us, but I let it go so that I could be prepared for our house guests. We had a large amount of company to come over, many people who'd never been to our house before, so it was good to host some new people. We had an absolutely good time. My house was full of my family - my mom, sister, both daughters, niece, my daughter's in-laws, old church members from Houston, and a bunch of friends. It was a great time. I hadn't been that happy in a long time and I was loving it. In addition to us having a cake for my niece's graduation, my husband even surprised all the mothers and bought a Mother's Day cake with all our names on it. He gave me a nice, large balloon bouquet too.

But the happiness and joy I experienced that day was short lived. After all the company left, my husband left also. Since I was home alone, I decided to take a nap until my husband and daughter returned. But my husband called me on the phone to express his disgust about one of the guests who had come to the party: a male college friend of our youngest daughter. I had to take a call from my other daughter who left her purse, so I couldn't continue the conversation. When he returned home, a minor discussion regarding the guest went from a disagreement to an argument, which escalated into us having an intense, physical altercation, which scared me tremendously. Unfortunately, this wasn't our first physical altercation. We'd had seven before that.

Our daughter had called the police for five of those altercations, resulting in them saying they would take us to jail if they had to come again. The one we had in February was a pretty bad one that ended with me calling the police. They asked me if I had struck him and I said yes, to which they responded they'd have to take me to jail. I told them if I had to go to jail in order for him to go, I'd be willing to do that. However, when my husband left the house, which was a Saturday, he stayed gone for several days. As a matter of fact, that Sunday morning, he snuck into the house while I was asleep to get clothes for church and sung with the Praise & Worship team during service. That disgusted me.But this last altercation was the worst. It was different and he was different. It seemed as if he really wanted to do some serious harm to me and like he even may have wanted to kill me. In fact, when my daughter attempted to call the police, he stopped her.

After the devastating altercation, I ran upstairs and locked myself in the bathroom, and cried heavily while trying to nurse the wounds that I received. He must have thought that I was calling the police, so to avoid the police he left the house. I, then, barricaded myself in one of the guest bedrooms. The next day, I awoke to realize that he stayed gone that night. I no longer wanted to endure this type of treatment from this *"Man of God."*

I called the Domestic Violence Hotline for assistance. They told me my options and stated they would assist me with whatever decision I made. I pondered the several options presented to me. The options I had before me were: go to a women's shelter, file a Protective Order of Abuse and remain in the home, or leave altogether. My sister had not yet left DC to go back to Houston following the graduation celebration, so I called her because I needed someone to talk it through with. But she said I had to be the one to make a decision about what I was going to do. Then she began to pray. During the prayer, she switched to praying in tongues, and while she was doing so, I heard strongly in my spirit, like it was a 10-ton weight dropping, "Leave!" I began to cry because I knew that was going to be a huge step to take. I told her what I heard and hung up to call the Domestic Violence hotline back. They assisted in facilitating my departure from my home that day by purchasing a one-way ticket for me to go to Houston.

I packed 2 suitcases with clothes, shoes, and a few essentials, not knowing how long I'd be gone. I'm still gone, and although I have since visited the house on several occasions to get some more clothes and shoes, there is still a huge amount I left behind. In essence, I left my marriage, my home, and all of the material things for my freedom.

There are a few things I found out after I left the church. I recognized that day in church when the Pastor and I had the confrontation about him violating me as an opportunity for him to repent for his actions during our time of indiscretions and release me. But he refused. In fact, he insisted on denying his involvement with me and, in order to cover his butt, the Pastor told my husband that I was making false accusations against him. Until then, I still hadn't told my husband anything, but when my husband confronted me with that, I felt the release to tell him everything. I told him everything detailed in this book about my affair with the Pastor.

I even confessed to another affair that I had, but I didn't tell him about the two church members. I didn't want to tell him about my affairs with the church members because they all go to church together, and I felt like I wanted to protect them and their families. However, I've since gotten the revelation that protecting them and their families dishonored my husband because my first priority should have been to protect our family. I've repented to God for it.

Of course when my husband confronted the Pastor, he

once again denied it and blamed everything on me. In spite of all of that, my husband still remained a member of that church, long after finding out about the Pastor's indiscretions with me.

I also learned that during the time I was there after our confrontation, the Pastor told the church's security team that they needed to watch me and my husband, especially me because I was "unstable." He even assigned a female security member specifically to me. He told her that he knew she was crazy enough to handle me if I got out of line. This was disturbing to hear and I'm sure this probably made the young lady quite uncomfortable to know that she had to come to church, not to receive the word of God, but to "watch" a member in case she got out of line. I thought that was so funny, actually, especially when I did not exhibit any of the signs of which I was made out to be. I was nowhere near being unstable. I had a total sound mind and self-control. It just goes to show the lengths this Pastor was going through to cover his actions, which I've since learned as behavior of a narcissist.

I literally went into the church and went straight to my seat, worshipped during praise & worship, sat during the sermon while ignoring it and impatiently waiting for it to be over, and went straight to my car to wait for my husband after services while he fellowshipped. As a matter of fact, I was extremely free, I just needed a little bit more freedom and to break out of the bondage of that church. For the life of me, I couldn't understand why the Pastor didn't just tell me to leave or even tell my husband to tell me to leave. I would have gladly left the church since that is what I was wanting anyway. My husband was the only reason I was still going there. I submitted to him to keep *some* peace in my household.

Even after having all the blame put on me, I stayed silent. I remained silent until finally, as I stated earlier, on August 25, 2018 while at a conference in Dallas, TX, God gave me the release to tell my story.

CHAPTER 14

Be Free Indeed

Once again, why did I write this story?

Many people, especially Christians, Believers, or "church people" have lived in bondage to secrets we hold from either things we've done in our lives or things that were done to us. God wants us to live in total liberty — *the state of not being imprisoned or enslaved.* Past mistakes can imprison and enslave us, especially in our thoughts. They can hold us back from accomplishing things we should be doing in life, or living out our purpose and full potential. When you have overcome something that you have gone through in life, and especially have received deliverance from it, it is your duty to share it and help someone else so that they too may be able to overcome obstacles in life, be free from strongholds and bondages, get deliverance, and live in complete freedom. It is my heart's desire that others be truly free in their lives.

Many people are still bound to sin because they don't know how to get out and that's because they don't get to hear about someone else's deliverance from sin and how they came out of it to be restored by God's love, forgiveness, grace, and mercy. Complete transparency is something that is missing from the church. From this story you can tell that I was completely bound to sin and lust. Since then, I've received deliverance and I live in complete freedom from the spirit of perversion. Therefore, because I have walked through this, I can help someone else who is struggling and really wants to be free from sexual sins. That is one of the main reasons why I can be courageous, bold, and free in sharing my transparent truth.

We also have to know that we can be free from shame of past sins and mistakes. Our sins and mistakes are covered under the blood of Jesus. We don't have to live in shame because man can't condemn us once God has forgiven us. People may try to condemn us, but if God doesn't, what man says doesn't matter. A lot of people, especially in the church, are still walking around with shame when they have been made free. I am not ashamed to have told this story or any story I've written pertaining to my past. I am free and I don't care what people may think of me after reading this. I did what I did but I am NOT what I did. I Am Who God says I am; Forgiven and Free!

If you have been suffering in silence from the things you've done or what has been done to you, be free. Get the help that you need. Seek spiritual counsel, mental health counsel, and also spend time praying, reading the Bible, and listening to teaching and preaching of the word of God. You have to saturate yourself with the word. You have to take the time out and make having a pure heart, and living a holy and free lifestyle, a priority. Once you do that, everything you do will start to fall into place.

Suffer no more. Speak up and speak out. Don't be afraid of man. Don't let man tell you to let the past be the past and to keep silent about it. That is a lie. The story of David sleeping with Bathsheba, a married woman, and having her husband Uriah killed had been done in the past, but God still brought the Prophet Nathan to speak to him about it.

The only reason why we know of this story is because God had it to be written in the bible in 2 Samuel chapters 11 and 12. From that story, we've learned of repentance, reverence, and heartfelt worship because of the testimony of David in the book of Psalms.

Again, do not be afraid to share your story because of man. If God is for you, who can be against you (Romans 8:31). If the Lord is with me; I will not be afraid. What can man do to me? (Psalm 118:6). If God is telling you to speak out and tell your story, either for the sake of deliverance or to help someone else, obey as He commanded the Prophet Jeremiah in Jeremiah 1:7-8: *"But the Lord said to me, do not say, 'I am too young.' You must go to everyone I send you to and say whatever I command you, do not be afraid of them, for I am with you and will rescue you declares the Lord."*

The behaviors detailed in this story were unrighteous and unacceptable, but I can guarantee some of the behaviors are relatable to many people. The stronghold of infidelity in the church is a vicious one, but we must be free from these sins continuing in the church body. Speaking out about them opens the door for people to get help, deliverance, and for these sins to be uprooted out of the church, and for these types of strongholds to be torn down. It is one we don't want to talk about or deal with. We pretend it doesn't exist because these are men and women of God. Christians. Preachers and Leaders. Respected pillars of society and the church community.

This vicious cycle ruins families, careers, purposes, dreams, and society. It puts a mark and a stain on you that's sometimes hard for some to overlook when you've actually gotten free from that past. It is a cycle that must stop. It's been going on far too long. It has ruined way too many people, reputations, ministries, and more importantly, it's suppressing God's glory from fully going forth. There has to be open, transparent conversation so the strongholds and cycles can be exposed, seen for what they are, and attacked so that we, "The church," can stop it.

There are people in the church who are victims of this behavior and who are being hurt over and over again, and they too are suffering in silence and need to be free. They are being hurt by broken and hurting people. True healing and deliverance needs to take place in the church and in families so that these cycles can be broken from bloodlines. Someone needs to be the bloodline breaker of repetitive sinful habits and behaviors from traveling from generation to generation.

Jesus Christ has set us free from sin by His death on the cross. He wants us to truly live in that freedom from sin, strongholds, bondages, and demonic influences. Since freedom belongs to those who believe in Jesus Christ, BE FREE INDEED! I've been made free, so it is my freedom that has called me to be a voice for those suffering in silence to sin, brokenness, hurts, strongholds, depression, or pain that they have experienced as recipients or perpetrators.

In Conclusion, I must again emphasize that we have to be careful about who we let sow and plant into us and be careful about what they plant or sow into us. Literally, through my inappropriate interactions with the Pastor and the other members, you saw what was being sown into me and the bad harvest I reaped. The lesson to be learned here is that it doesn't matter who is doing the sowing, stop them, rebuke them, correct them, get away from them if the seeds are contrary to the word of God or unwholesome conversation is being sown into you. You have to protect yourself from reaping the wrong type of harvest in your life. You also must stop yourself from allowing bad seeds to be sown into you and from accepting them because of your feelings about who they came from. Also, be mindful of what you are planting or sowing into other people. You don't want to be responsible for the negative harvest they reap because of seeds you've sown.

Walk in the spirit so that you won't fulfill the lust of the flesh (Galatians 5:16). Meaning, to not fulfill the lust of your flesh or the lust of someone else's flesh, always stay at a place of walking/living in the spirit. Always live righteously and holy. And if you happen to mess up, repent and turn away so that you won't do it again. Make a decision that you don't want to do anything that is not pleasing to God. You are to be a witness and representation of Jesus in the earth. You can't minister to someone spiritually and lead them down the wrong path at the same time. They just don't go together. One is going to dominate; the flesh or the spirit but they can't co-exist. You saw in this story, although he was my Pastor and was ministering to me, either by way of pulpit or personal counsel, he also ministered to my flesh with fleshly things and my flesh dominated over the spirit.

It is my prayer that you are not left with judgment or condemnation now that you have read this story, but through the eyes of the spirit, you have received healing, wholeness, deliverance, restoration, and more importantly freedom.

Be Free - **John 8:32** *And you shall know the truth, and the truth shall make you free.*

Be Free Indeed - **John 8:36** *If the Son therefore shall make you free, you shall be free indeed.*

This story is about what I did, but not who I am. I Am not what I did, **"I Am Free!"**

Free from the sin
Free from the guilt
Free from the shame
Free from the bondage
Free from the conviction
Even **Free** from the condemnation, persecution, and judgment that may come as a result of writing this story.

Free Indeed!

Prayer of Freedom

Heavenly Father, I thank you for your word and the power of your word. I thank you that the scriptures say that the truth shall make me free and who the Son sets free is free indeed. Therefore, I pray that as I have come in contact with the truth of your word, freedom is mine. I am free in Jesus Christ because he is my Lord & Savior. Therefore, I will no longer be bound by my past and I will not let the enemy hold me hostage in my thoughts because of my past. I decree and declare that I am free from bondages and strongholds and I will not let anything hinder my freedom. I am forgiven and I walk in the liberty of forgiveness that God has given me. The blood of Jesus has cleansed me of all unrighteousness and I have received God's love, grace, and mercy so that I can live a life that is free of sin, guilt, and condemnation. I thank you Father that I am free, free indeed!

NOTES

1. Terri Savelle Foy, *Breaking Soul Ties*
www.terri.com

2. Kris Vallotton, *7 Signs of an Unhealthy Soul Tie*
www.krisvallotton.com

3. *What are the Job Duties of a Pastor?* Learn.org

About the Author

Wendi Hayman is an author, publisher, entrepreneur, speaker, and mother. She is called to impact and advance the Kingdom as a prophetic voice of purpose. Her story is a long and winding road from the pole, to the pew, to God's purpose for her life. For many years, Wendi lived with guilt and embarrassment of past experiences as an exotic dancer and would not share her story with anyone. After finding freedom in Christ, she emerged out of hiding and moved forward beyond her past to empower women around the globe.

Work with Wendi
Wendi is a creative powerhouse, who uses her passions to help others and advance the kingdom of God. As a speaker and writer, Wendi works closely with ministry leaders, aspiring authors and mission-driven entrepreneurs in a variety of ways.

Speaking
Women of all ages relate to Wendi's transparent truth, in her book Blind Ambition, of seeking validity in the wrong places until finally discovering her purpose. Wendi has shared platforms and stages with Powerhouses, Influencers, and Celebrities – Tressa Smallwood, Publisher & Executive Film Producer; Tamara Hush Lee, Celebrity Stylist; Dr. Kym Lee, Celebrity Makeup Artist; Carla Watson, Confidence Life Coach; Jamie Foster-Brown, Founder of Sister 2 Sister Magazine; Traci Braxton, Singer & Actress; Arnicia V, Celebrity Human Resource Executive; Dr. Missy Johnson, Fearless Women Rock Life Coach. Wendi speaks on

the following topics to women and young adult audiences in business, entrepreneurship, schools, community and women's organizations.
• Recovering from Life's Pitfalls
• Giving God the Best You (Purpose & Vision Talk)
• Sharing your Testimony, Confidently & Boldly

Ghostwriting and Publishing
As the Creative Director of Glory to Glory Publications, LLC, Wendi enjoys helping aspiring authors write and publish their books. She has created a stress-free book consulting, co-writing, and ghostwriting process to take authors from book idea to implementation.

Send booking inquiries to: wendihayman@gmail.com

For more information, visit online at:
www.wendihayman.com
wendihayman@gmail.com
glorytoglorypublications@gmail.com
Facebook: Wendi Hayman
Instagram: @wendihayman
Periscope: Wendi Hayman
Twitter: Hayman_Wendi

OTHER BOOKS BY WENDI

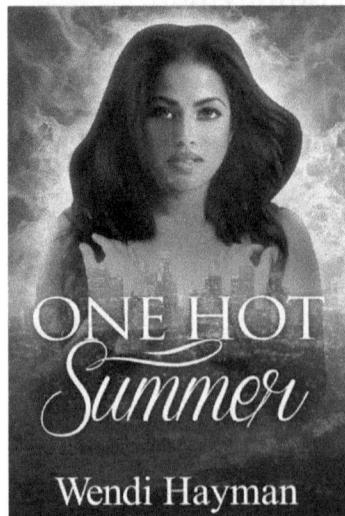

www.ingramcontent.com/pod-product-compliance
Lightning Source LLC
Chambersburg PA
CBHW061738020426
42331CB00006B/1288